© 2023 by ADISA Publishing AB, Sweden

All Scripture quotations, unless otherwise indicated, are taken from The Holy Bible, English Standard Version (ESV), copyright © 2001 by Crossway Bibles, a publishing ministry of Good News Publishers. Used by permission. All rights reserved.

First Edition. Every attempt has been made to trace and acknowledge copyright. The opinions and content are the author's own. Neither the Publisher nor the author makes any representation about the issues herein.

INTRODUCTION

In life's journey, few relationships carry the weight of significance and profoundness quite like marriage. a sacred union, a lifelong commitment, and a beautiful tapestry are woven with love, trust, and faith between a man and a woman. Yet, even the strongest marriages require nurturing, understanding, and intentional effort to thrive and flourish through life's seasons. Weaving together the threads of devotion, communication, intimacy, and spirituality, "Bound Together in Love: a Marriage Devotional For Couples" invites you to embark on a transformative voyage, hand in hand with your spouse, exploring the depths of your love for one another and your devotion to God.

Within these pages, you will discover a treasury of wisdom, encouragement, and practical guidance aimed at fortifying the foundation of your marriage, "Bound Together in Love" is not just a book; it is an immersive experience carefully crafted to foster unity, understanding, and a deeper connection between you and your spouse. You will embark on a new discovery, reflection, and growth chapter each week. As you dive into Scripture, engage with thought-provoking devotions, explore meaningful questions together, and participate in fun activities along with enriching tasks, you will be guided toward a richer appreciation of the divine gift that is your marriage.

"Bound Together In Love" is not a mere read-and-discuss book; it is a keepsake that will become an integral part of your marriage journey. As you complete each week's devotional, reflect on your experiences, and pray together, this workbook will accumulate the essence of your shared growth and love. In the years to come, you will be able to revisit the pages, reminiscing about the transformative moments that have made your bond stronger.

This is your chance to reaffirm your commitment to one another, reignite the passion, and draw closer to God as the center of your union. Whether you have been married for decades or are just starting your life together, "Bound Together in Love" offers a promise of renewal, and you are encouraged to approach each week with an open heart along with an eagerness to learn and grow.

Together, you will face challenges, savor joys, and discover new dimensions of your love that you never thought possible. May this journey bring you closer together as a couple and strengthen your bond with the Almighty, for in love and faith, all things are possible.

TABLE OF CONTENT

HOW-TO GUIDE

Welcome to "Bound Together In Love - a Marriage Devotional for Couples." This comprehensive guide is designed to help couples strengthen their relationship by deepening their spiritual connection and nurturing their love through meaningful activities, reflections, and prayers. In this guide, we will provide an overview of how to make the most of this workbook and enrich your marriage journey together.

1. Setting the Foundation

Before you begin the workbook, take some time as a couple to set clear intentions and goals for your marriage journey. Discuss why you chose to use this workbook, what you hope to gain from it, and the commitment you both have to grow together spiritually and emotionally.

2. Weekly Devotional Pieces

The heart of this workbook lies in the 52 weekly devotional pieces. Each week, set aside time to read the devotional together as a couple. Reflect on the Scriptures provided through the English Standard Version of the Bible, along with the devotion's message and the reflection questions. Share your thoughts, feelings, and insights openly with one another.

3. Embrace Gratitude

As you progress through the workbook, practice gratitude in your marriage. Make a habit of expressing appreciation for each other's efforts, love, and support. Regularly share things you appreciate about one another, both big and small.

4. Engage in Marriage Activities/Spiritual Practices

Each week, participate in either the marriage activity or spiritual practice suggested for that devotion. These activities are designed to promote communication, intimacy, and unity in your marriage. Embrace them with an open heart and a spirit of adventure.

5. Prioritize Quality Time

Make time for quality time together regularly. Plan date nights, outings, or activities that bring joy to both of you. Use these moments to strengthen your emotional connection and create lasting memories.

6. Nurture Spiritual Practice

Integrate prayer into your daily lives. Dedicate time to pray together, asking God's guidance, wisdom, and blessings on your marriage. Pray for each other's dreams, challenges, and growth.

7. Reflect on Your Journey

Periodically, take a moment to reflect on your marriage journey using the reflection questions provided in the devotions. Discuss your progress, celebrate your achievements, write down those thoughts for future reference in the space provided, and explore areas for growth.

8. Be Open and Vulnerable

Throughout this workbook, be open and vulnerable with each other. Share your thoughts, feelings, and fears honestly, creating a safe space for emotional intimacy and growth.

9. Celebrate Milestones

Celebrate the completion of each week's devotion. Acknowledge your commitment to the journey and the positive changes you see in your relationship.

10. Seek Support

If you encounter challenges or feel stuck during the workbook, don't hesitate to seek support. Consider seeking guidance from a trusted counselor or a spiritual mentor to help navigate any obstacles.

Conclusion

"Bound Together In Love - a Marriage Devotional for Couples" is a powerful tool for deepening your spiritual and emotional bond as a couple. Through the devotions, activities, and prayers, you will find a pathway to a more fulfilling and God-centered marriage. Embrace this journey with love, patience, and openness, and remember that growing together in love and faith is a beautiful gift that will last a lifetime. May God bless your marriage journey abundantly!

FOUNDATION OF LOVE

Scripture: Genesis 2:22

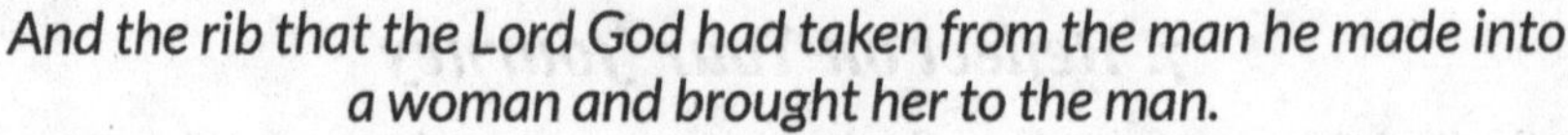

And the rib that the Lord God had taken from the man he made into a woman and brought her to the man.

Devotion:

Understanding God's design for marriage

In the beginning, when God created Adam, He saw that it was not good for man to be alone. Out of His deep love and perfect wisdom, God created a woman, Eve, to be a suitable helper and companion for Adam. This divine act of forming the first marriage laid the foundation for all future unions and established the sacred bond between husband and wife.

Marriage is not a mere human invention; it is a God-ordained institution. It reflects the deep unity and love shared within the Trinity itself, where the Father, Son, and Holy Spirit are in perfect harmony. As a result, marriage is designed to be a profound reflection of God's love and a beautiful partnership between two individuals, united by His grace and bound together by His plan.

Reflection:

Love is the cornerstone of marriage—a selfless, sacrificial, and unconditional love that echoes the love of Christ for His church. It goes beyond fleeting emotions and encompasses a commitment to cherish, honor, and support one another through all the seasons of life. Love is an intentional choice, demonstrated not just through words but through actions and deeds.

To better express love to your spouse, take time to truly understand their needs, desires, and dreams. Communicate openly and honestly, cultivating a safe space where vulnerability is embraced. Demonstrate kindness, patience, and forgiveness, recognizing that both of you are imperfect beings but united in love and grace. Seek opportunities to serve one another joyfully, knowing that small acts of love can have a profound impact on your marriage.

For Him

For Her

Marriage Activity:

This week, set aside intentional time to go on a "love adventure" with your spouse. Take a trip down memory lane and revisit the moments that brought you together - the first date, the proposal, or other special occasions. Share your feelings, recounting what you admire and cherish about each other. Capture these memories in a journal or a photo album so you can revisit them and add new memories over the years.

As you embark on this adventure, let it be a reminder of the love that has grown between you since the day you said, "I do." Celebrate the uniqueness of your marriage, knowing that it is a diving tapestry woven by God's hands.

PRAYER:

Gracious Heavenly Father,

We come before you today with hearts filled with gratitude for the gift of marriage. We thank you for designing this beautiful union, where two hearts become one in the presence of your love. As we reflect on the foundation of love in our marriage, we pray that you will strengthen the bonds that hold us together.

Lord, grant us the wisdom to understand that love is not just an emotion but a lifelong commitment to honor, respect, and cherish one another. Help us to be patient, kind, and selfless in our actions, putting the needs of our spouse before our own. May we always seek to build each other up, encouraging and supporting one another in both the highs and lows of life.

Lord, we ask for your guidance in navigating the challenges that come our way, knowing that with you as the cornerstone of our marriage, we can overcome any obstacle. Fill our hearts with forgiveness and understanding, so that we may extend grace to each other as you have extended grace to us.

Above all, Lord, we pray for a love that grows stronger each day—a love that reflects your unfailing and everlasting love. May our marriage be a shining example of your love to the world, bringing glory to your name.

In Jesus' name, we pray,

Amen

Closing Thoughts:

As you embark on this journey of love, remember that the foundation of your marriage is rooted in God's love and His divine plan. Embrace each day as a gift, an opportunity to grow closer to one another and to God. Let your love be a reflection of Christ's love for His church—a love that is selfless, sacrificial, and enduring. Together, hand in hand, build your marriage upon this firm foundation of love and let it be a beacon of hope and inspiration to those around you.

May this week mark the beginning of a transformative and love-filled journey where your marriage grows stronger with each passing day. May God's grace and presence be the guiding light in your hearts and your home.

COMMUNICATION

Scripture: Ephesians 4:29

Let no corrupting talk come out of your mouths, but only such as is good for building up, as fits the occasion, that it may give grace to those who hear.

Devotion:

Communication is the lifeblood of a healthy and thriving marriage. It is the bridge that connects two hearts, allowing understanding, empathy, and connection to flow freely. However, effective communication requires intentional effort, for it is not merely the words we speak but the attitude with which we share them that truly makes a difference.

In Ephesians 4:29, the Apostle Paul offers invaluable guidance on how we should communicate with our spouses. He reminds us to let go of harmful speech and replace it with words that build up, encourage, and benefit one another. Paul also emphasizes the importance of resolving conflict with kindness, compassion, and forgiveness. As we internalize these principles, we lay the foundation for a deeper and more profound connection with our spouses.

Reflection:

Take a moment to reflect on your communication patterns with your spouse. Are there areas that need improvement? Perhaps you've noticed times when arguments escalate or your discussions seem to fall into a pattern of misunderstanding. Maybe there are unresolved issues or pent-up emotions that hinder open and honest communication.

Identifying these areas is the first step toward fostering positive change in your marriage. As you pinpoint areas for improvement, approach them with grace and humility. Acknowledge that growth is a journey, and both you and your spouse will need patience and understanding along the way.

Now, make a plan to address these areas. Set aside dedicated time to talk openly with your spouse about your communication goals and challenges. Create a safe and non-judgmental space where each of you can express your thoughts and feelings honestly. Be attentive listeners, seeking to understand each other's perspectives without interrupting or jumping to conclusions.

Consider setting regular communication check-ins to discuss your progress and celebrate the victories, no matter how small. Be open to constructive feedback and be willing to adapt your approach as needed. Remember, this journey of improving communication is one you take together as a team, supporting and encouraging each other along the way.

For Him

For Her

Spiritual Practice:

This week, incorporate a spiritual practice to enhance your communication with your spouse. Begin by dedicating time to prayer, both individually and as a couple. Seek God's guidance in expressing your thoughts and emotions effectively. Ask Him to help you listen with empathy and respond with love, especially during challenging discussions.

PRAYER:

Gracious Heavenly Father,

We come before you today, seeking your guidance and wisdom as we seek to improve our communication in marriage. We acknowledge that our words have the power to either build up or tear down, and we desire to use them for good, edifying one another.

Lord, help us to let go of unwholesome talk, bitterness, and anger that may hinder our communication. Fill our hearts with kindness, compassion, and forgiveness so that our words and actions reflect your love for us. May we be quick to listen and slow to speak, showing empathy and understanding to each other.

Holy Spirit, we invite you into our conversations, knowing that you dwell within us as a source of wisdom and comfort. Guide our hearts and minds, so that we may communicate effectively, with words that benefit and bring blessing to one another.

Lord, we lift up our weaknesses and areas for improvement before you. Grant us the strength and perseverance to work together as a team, supporting and encouraging one another as we grow in our communication skills.

Above all, help us to honor you in our communication. May our words and interactions be a testimony of your love and grace, drawing us closer to each other and to you.

In Jesus' name, we pray,

Amen.

Closing Thoughts:

Improving communication in your marriage is a transformative journey that requires intentionality and God's guidance. As you practice effective communication with your spouse, may you experience a deeper connection, greater understanding, and a renewed sense of love and unity. Remember, your marriage is a reflection of God's love for His people. Through improved communication, you have the opportunity to showcase His grace and goodness to the world. May your commitment to enhancing communication be a testament to the power of God's love in your marriage journey.

TRUST AND FORGIVENESS

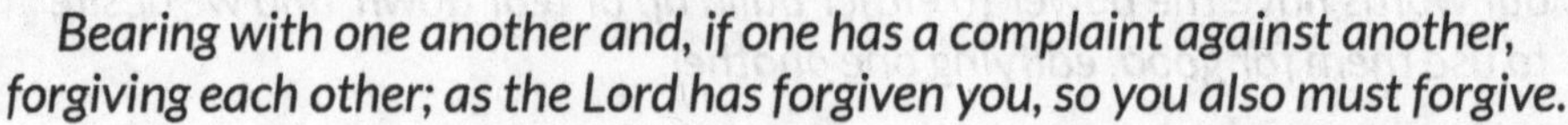

Scripture: Colossians 3:13

Bearing with one another and, if one has a complaint against another, forgiving each other; as the Lord has forgiven you, so you also must forgive.

Devotion:

Trust and forgiveness are the bedrock of a strong and resilient marriage. Just as the foundation provides stability and support to a building, trust, and forgiveness form the basis of a loving and enduring union. In Colossians 3:13, we are reminded of the divine mandate to bear with one another and to forgive, mirroring the gracious forgiveness we have received from the Lord.

Marriage is a journey that involves two imperfect individuals, each with their own flaws and vulnerabilities. At times, misunderstandings, mistakes, and hurts may challenge the trust between spouses. However, it is crucial to recognize that no relationship is immune to trials, and what truly matters is how we navigate these challenges together.

In the face of trust issues or hurt, forgiveness becomes a powerful healing agent. When we extend forgiveness, we break down the walls that divide us and create space for reconciliation and restoration. True forgiveness is not a one-time event but a continuous practice of letting go of resentment, healing wounds, and choosing to love anew.

Reflection:

Take time this week to have an open and honest conversation with your spouse about any lingering trust issues that may be present in your marriage. Create a safe and non-judgmental space where both of you can express your feelings and concerns without fear of reproach. As you share your hearts with each other, listen attentively and empathetically, seeking to understand each other's perspectives.

Remember that rebuilding trust is a joint effort that requires vulnerability, transparency, and patience. Be willing to take responsibility for any actions that may have caused hurt, and demonstrate genuine remorse. Acknowledge the impact of the hurt and commit to making amends and changing behaviors if necessary.

As you discuss ways to rebuild trust, consider setting clear boundaries and expectations to prevent future issues. Establish open lines of communication and be intentional about nurturing a culture of trust and emotional safety in your marriage.

Marriage Activity:

This week, engage in a trust-building activity that allows you both to deepen your connection and foster trust in your relationship. One such activity is writing heartfelt letters to each other, expressing your love, appreciation, and commitment. Use this opportunity to share your feelings, dreams, and hopes for your future together.

Alternatively, plan a fun and adventurous activity that requires teamwork and collaboration. This could be anything from cooking a meal together to trying a new hobby or sport. As you navigate this activity as a team, you will not only build trust but also create joyful memories that strengthen your bond.

PRAYER:

Gracious and Merciful Father,

We come before you today, seeking your guidance and strength as we journey towards deeper trust and forgiveness in our marriage. We acknowledge that forgiveness is not always easy, and rebuilding trust takes time and effort. Yet, we trust in your transformative power to heal and restore.

Lord, we lay before you any hurt or mistrust that may be lingering in our hearts. We ask for the courage to face these challenges head-on, acknowledging our weaknesses and vulnerabilities. Help us to extend forgiveness to each other as you have forgiven us, setting aside any bitterness or resentment.

Father, grant us the grace to bear with one another, recognizing that we are both on a journey of growth and redemption. Help us to be patient with each other's shortcomings and to offer grace and understanding in difficult times.

As we embark on activities to rebuild trust, we pray that you will be the unseen guest in our conversations and interactions. Guide us to communicate with love and respect, being open and honest with one another.

Above all, Lord, we pray for hearts that are receptive to forgiveness. Fill us with your love, so that we may forgive wholeheartedly and experience the freedom that comes with letting go of past hurts.

We commit our marriage to your hands, trusting that you are the source of all healing and restoration. May our journey of trust and forgiveness draw us closer to each other and to you.

In Jesus' name, we pray,

Amen.

Closing Thoughts:

Trust and forgiveness are integral to the health and longevity of any marriage. As you navigate the complexities of rebuilding trust and extending forgiveness, remember that God's grace is more than sufficient to heal any wounds and mend any brokenness. Trust in His timing and guidance as you seek to nurture a culture of trust and grace in your marriage.

Embrace this week as an opportunity to grow closer as a couple, deepening your connection through open communication, forgiveness, and vulnerability. Be patient with yourselves and with each other, knowing that rebuilding trust is a journey that requires time, effort, and God's guiding hand.

May you experience the transformative power of trust and forgiveness in your marriage, and may your love continue to grow stronger each day, reflecting the boundless love and forgiveness of our Heavenly Father.

INTIMACY

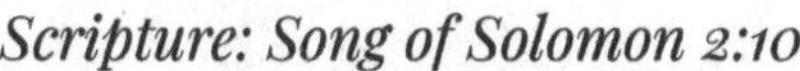

Scripture: Song of Solomon 2:10

My beloved speaks and says to me: "Arise, my love, my beautiful one, and come away."

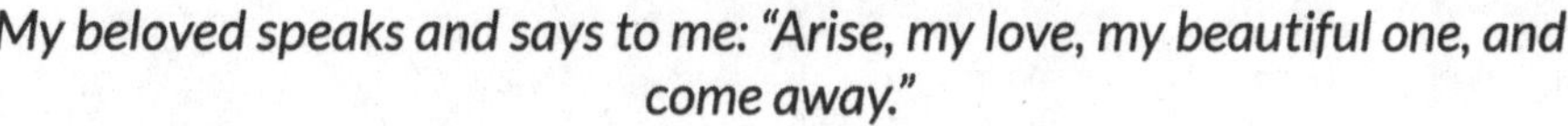

Devotion:

In the beautiful poetry of the Song of Solomon, we find an expression of deep emotional and physical intimacy between two lovers. This ancient text captures the essence of love, desire, and affection within the context of marriage. It reminds us that intimacy is not confined to the physical realm alone but encompasses the profound emotional connection that binds two souls together.

Cultivating intimacy is a sacred journey in marriage - a journey of vulnerability, trust, and selflessness. Emotional intimacy involves open communication, active listening, and a genuine desire to understand and support one another. It is the foundation on which physical intimacy flourishes, deepening the bond between spouses and enhancing the overall closeness in the marriage.

Reflection:

This week, take time to reflect on the emotional and physical aspects of intimacy in your marriage. Engage in open and honest conversations with your spouse about your desires, needs, and boundaries within the context of intimacy. Create a safe space where both of you feel comfortable expressing your feelings and preferences.

Remember that intimacy is a shared journey, and understanding each other's desires and boundaries is crucial to fostering a fulfilling and loving connection. Be attentive listeners, seeking to empathize with each other's perspectives and feelings. Embrace vulnerability and be willing to share your thoughts openly, knowing that your spouse is your confidant and ally in this sacred journey.

As you share your desires and boundaries, approach the conversation with gentleness and respect. Be mindful of each other's sensitivities and feelings, ensuring that the dialogue remains loving and supportive. Mutual understanding and mutual respect form the pillars upon which emotional and physical intimacy thrive.

FOR HER

Spiritual Practice:

Incorporate a spiritual practice that invites God into the intimate aspect of your marriage. Set aside time for prayer together, seeking God's blessing on the physical aspect of your relationship. Express your gratitude to God for the gift of intimacy and the opportunity to grow closer as a couple.

As you pray, invite God to be the center of your marital intimacy, guiding your actions, desires, and expressions of love. Ask Him to help you view physical intimacy as an act of love and self-giving, cherishing the sacredness of the gift you share with one another.

PRAYER:

Heavenly Father,

We come before you with hearts full of gratitude for the gift of intimacy in our marriage. We thank You for creating us as physical and emotional beings, capable of experiencing love and connection in such a profound way.

Lord, we invite you into the intimate aspect of our relationship. We ask for your blessing on the physical bond we share as husband and wife. May our physical expressions of love be a reflection of the love and grace you have shown us.

We pray for sensitivity and understanding as we share our desires and boundaries with one another. Help us to be attentive listeners and compassionate confidants, nurturing a culture of open communication and mutual respect.

Father, guide us in embracing vulnerability and trust as we deepen our emotional intimacy. May we be each other's safe haven, where we can share our deepest thoughts and feelings without fear of judgment.

Above all, Lord, we invite you to be the center of our intimacy. May our physical expressions of love be an act of worship and a celebration of the covenant we share. Help us to cherish and honor the gift of intimacy you have bestowed upon us.

As we walk this sacred journey together, may we be guided by your love and grace, nurturing the emotional and physical bond that unites us.

In Jesus' name, we pray,

Amen.

Closing Thoughts:

Intimacy is a multifaceted and deeply meaningful aspect of marriage. As you cultivate emotional and physical intimacy in your relationship, remember that it is a journey of exploration, growth, and mutual love. Seek God's guidance and blessing on this sacred aspect of your marriage, knowing that He is the source of all love and connection.

Approach intimacy as an opportunity to draw closer to your spouse emotionally and physically, cherishing the unique bond you share. May this week be a time of vulnerability, open communication, and mutual respect, fostering a deeper sense of intimacy and unity in your marriage.

Remember that God's design for intimacy is rooted in love and self-giving. As you embrace this divine plan, you will discover that intimacy becomes a beautiful and enriching aspect of your marital journey, drawing you closer together and closer to the heart of God.

CONFLICT RESOLUTION

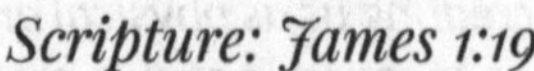

Scripture: James 1:19

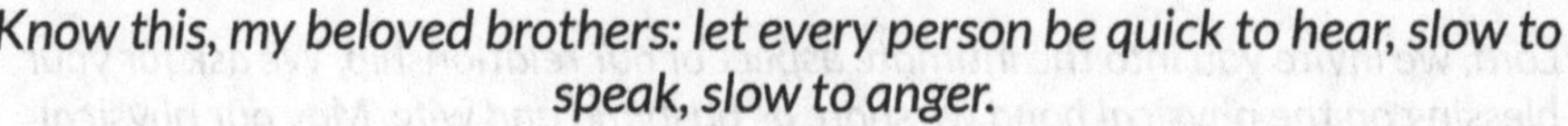

Know this, my beloved brothers: let every person be quick to hear, slow to speak, slow to anger.

Devotion:

Conflict is an inevitable part of any relationship, including marriage. However, how we handle conflict can make all the difference in the health and growth of our marriage. In James 1:19, we are encouraged to be quick to listen, slow to speak, and slow to become angry. These words offer invaluable wisdom on how to navigate conflicts with grace and compassion.

Healthy conflict resolution requires a foundation of mutual respect, humility, and a commitment to understanding each other's perspectives. It involves setting aside defensiveness and ego, embracing vulnerability, and working together to find resolutions that honor both individuals' feelings and needs.

Reflection:

Reflect on your approach to conflict resolution in your marriage. Are there patterns of communication that hinder effective resolution? Do disagreements tend to escalate into arguments without reaching a resolution? Take an honest look at how you and your spouse engage in conflict and seek opportunities for growth.

One essential aspect of conflict resolution is learning to listen actively. When we listen with an open heart and a willingness to understand, we create a space where both individuals feel heard and validated. Practice active listening by giving your spouse your full attention, maintaining eye contact, and refraining from interrupting. Seek to understand their emotions, concerns, and desires without judgment or criticism.

As you engage in discussions about areas of disagreement, avoid blame and defensiveness. Instead, focus on using "I" statements to express your feelings and perspectives. For example, say, "I feel hurt when..." or "I would appreciate it if..." This approach helps to foster empathy and understanding, setting the stage for a constructive and productive conversation.

Marriage Activity:

Engage in a conflict resolution activity that allows both of you to practice healthy communication and understanding. Consider setting aside dedicated time to discuss a recent disagreement or an ongoing issue that needs resolution.

During this activity, commit to using active listening skills and "I" statements. Encourage each other to express their thoughts and emotions honestly without fear of judgment. As you listen, resist the urge to interrupt or become defensive. Instead, seek to understand your spouse's perspective fully.

As you engage in the conversation, be mindful of your tone and body language, striving to communicate with respect and love. Remember, the goal is not to "win" the argument but to find a resolution that strengthens your connection and honors both individuals' feelings.

PRAYER:

Heavenly Father,

We come before you with hearts full of gratitude for the gift of marriage, where we can grow in love and understanding through conflicts and challenges. We acknowledge that conflicts are a natural part of relationships, and we seek your wisdom and guidance in handling them with grace and compassion.

Lord, we pray for the humility to be quick to listen and slow to speak. Teach us to set aside our own agendas and egos, so that we may create a safe space for honest and open communication. Help us to be attentive listeners, seeking to understand each other's perspectives without judgment.

Father, we recognize that anger can often cloud our judgment and lead to hurtful words and actions. We pray for the ability to manage our emotions, responding to conflicts with love and patience rather than reacting in anger.

Grant us the strength to embrace vulnerability during disagreements, as we strive to share our feelings and thoughts honestly. May we be receptive to each other's needs and desires, seeking resolutions that honor and respect both individuals.

Above all, Lord, we seek your wisdom in finding resolutions that reflect your righteousness. May the way we handle conflicts in our marriage be a testament to your love and grace, drawing us closer to each other and to you.

As we engage in conflict resolution, may your presence be our guide, comforting us in difficult moments and empowering us to navigate conflicts with wisdom and understanding.

In Jesus' name, we pray,

Amen

Closing Thoughts:

Conflict resolution is a skill that requires practice, patience, and a heart that seeks understanding and empathy. As you strive to handle conflicts with grace and compassion in your marriage, remember that every disagreement presents an opportunity for growth and deeper connection.

Approach conflict as an opportunity to learn more about each other and to strengthen the bond you share. Seek God's wisdom in handling conflicts, relying on His love and guidance to navigate difficult conversations with grace and humility.

May this week be a time of growth and healing in your marriage as you practice healthy conflict resolution and build a foundation of love, respect, and understanding that will sustain your relationship for years to come.

FINANCES

Scripture: Proverbs 22:7

The rich rules over the poor, and the borrower is the slave of the lender.

Devotion:

Finances play a significant role in our lives, including our marriages. How we manage money can impact the stability, unity, and peace within our relationship. In Proverbs 22:7, we are reminded of the importance of financial responsibility and avoiding debt that can become a burden. As a couple, it is crucial to align your financial goals and priorities, working together to build a secure and harmonious financial future.

Aligning financial goals involves open and honest communication about your individual attitudes toward money, spending habits, and long-term aspirations. It also requires embracing a shared vision for your finances - one that promotes unity and mutual support.

Reflection:

Take time to reflect on your current financial situation as a couple. Are there areas that need improvement or discussions that you have been avoiding? Begin by having an open conversation about your financial goals and the values that underpin them.

Discuss the importance of budgeting and how you can create a financial plan that reflects your shared vision for the future. Be willing to make compromises and prioritize your financial responsibilities together.

During your conversation, consider setting financial goals that are both short-term and long-term. Short-term goals may include creating an emergency fund, paying off debts, or saving for a specific purchase. Long-term goals may involve saving for retirement, a down payment on a home, or your children's education.

Spiritual Practice:

Incorporate the spiritual practice of tithing (10% of your income) into your church if you have not already done so. At the same time, integrate prayer into your financial journey as a couple. Dedicate time each day to pray together, seeking God's wisdom and guidance in managing your finances.

Pray for the strength to resist financial temptations and avoid unnecessary debt. Ask God to grant you both the discipline and self-control to spend wisely and save diligently.

Pray for contentment and gratitude for what you have, learning to be good stewards of the resources God has entrusted to you. Seek His direction in how you can use your finances to bless others and contribute to causes that align with your values.

Heavenly Father,

We come before you today, acknowledging that you are the source of all provision and wisdom. We thank you for the resources you have blessed us with and for bringing us together in marriage.

Lord, as we reflect on our finances, we recognize that managing money can be a source of stress and tension. We pray for your wisdom and guidance as we align our financial goals and priorities.

Grant us the ability to communicate openly and honestly about our attitudes toward money and our financial aspirations. Help us to be good stewards of the resources you have entrusted to us, making wise financial decisions that honor you and support our shared vision for the future.

Father, we lift up our financial goals to you—both short-term and long-term. May our financial journey be one of unity, mutual support, and celebration of our achievements.

We also pray for the strength to resist the allure of unnecessary debt. Help us to live within our means and to avoid financial burdens that can strain our marriage.

Lord, teach us to be content with what we have and to find joy in the simple blessings of life. May our finances be used to bless others and to support causes that reflect your heart.

Above all, we seek your wisdom and discernment in managing our finances. May every financial decision we make align with your will and bring glory to your name.

In Jesus' name, we pray,

Amen.

Closing Thoughts:

As you align your financial goals and priorities in your marriage, remember that this is a journey you take together, as a team. Embrace open communication, honesty, and compromise as you work toward financial stability and unity.

Make prayer an integral part of your financial journey, seeking God's wisdom and guidance in managing your resources. Trust that with God as your guide, you can overcome financial challenges and build a secure and prosperous future together.

May this week be a time of growth and unity as you align your financial goals, celebrate your achievements, and seek God's blessings on your financial journey as a couple.

BUILDING A STRONG SPIRITUAL FOUNDATION

Scripture: Psalm 127:1

Unless the Lord builds the house, those who build it labor in vain. Unless the Lord watches over the city, the watchman stays awake in vain.

Devotion:

A strong and lasting marriage requires a solid foundation. Just as a house built on a strong and sturdy foundation can withstand storms, a marriage built on a strong spiritual foundation can weather the trials and challenges that life brings. Psalm 127:1 reminds us that unless the Lord is at the center of our marriage, our efforts will be in vain.

Prioritizing spiritual growth as a couple involves intentionally seeking God's presence and guidance in every aspect of your relationship. It means nurturing your individual relationships with Him while also cultivating a shared spiritual journey that strengthens your bond and deepens your love.

Reflection:

Take time to reflect on your spiritual journey as a couple. Discuss how you can grow closer to God individually and as a team. Consider ways to incorporate spiritual practices into your daily lives and make room for God to play a central role in your marriage.

Explore opportunities for spiritual growth together, such as attending religious services, reading and studying the Bible together, participating in prayer and meditation, or engaging in acts of service to others. Seek to create a home environment where God's presence is welcomed and where His love and grace are extended to one another.

Marriage Activity:

Embark on a spiritual adventure together. Set aside time for a "spiritual date night" where you engage in activities that nourish your soul and deepen your connection with God.

Visit a place of worship together or participate in a virtual spiritual event or retreat. Spend time reading and discussing a spiritual book or devotion that resonates with both of you. Engage in a joint prayer session, expressing your hopes, dreams, and concerns to God as a couple.

Use this time to share your spiritual insights, ask questions, and encourage one another in your faith. This activity is not only a way to grow spiritually together but also a beautiful opportunity to draw closer to each other as you connect on a deeper, soulful level.

PRAYER:

Heavenly Father,

We come before you with hearts full of gratitude for the love and unity you have bestowed upon our marriage. We acknowledge that our relationship is built on your love and grace, and we seek to deepen our spiritual foundation as a couple.

Lord, help us to prioritize our spiritual growth as individuals and as a team. May our love for you and our commitment to following your ways be evident in every aspect of our lives.

Guide us as we explore ways to grow spiritually together. Show us how to create a home that reflects your love and presence, where we can seek refuge and strength in you.

As we engage in spiritual practices together, draw us closer to you and to each other. May our faith journey be a shared adventure, filled with moments of inspiration and revelation.

Father, we lift up our marriage to you, asking for your continued guidance and protection. Be the foundation of our relationship, and help us to build our lives together on the solid rock of your love and truth.

Teach us to be patient and compassionate with one another as we navigate the ups and downs of life. May our spiritual growth foster a deeper understanding and appreciation of each other.

We pray that our marriage will be a shining example of your love and grace to others, drawing them closer to you through our testimony.

In Jesus' name, we pray,

Amen.

Closing Thoughts:

Building a strong spiritual foundation in your marriage is a transformative journey that draws you closer to God and to each other. As you prioritize spiritual growth, remember that it is not just an individual pursuit but a shared adventure.

Use this week as a time to explore ways to grow spiritually together, nurturing your relationship with God and each other. Embrace prayer as a central practice, seeking God's guidance and presence in your lives and marriage.

May your commitment to spiritual growth deepen your love, strengthen your bond, and bring glory to God as you build a solid foundation for a lasting and fulfilling marriage.

GRATITUDE AND APPRECIATION

Scripture: 1 Thessalonians 5:18

Give thanks in all circumstances; for this is the will of God in Christ Jesus for you.

Devotion:

Gratitude is a powerful force that can transform our lives, including our marriages. When we cultivate a spirit of gratitude, we shift our focus from what we lack to what we have, and we begin to see the abundance of blessings that surrounds us. In 1 Thessalonians 5:18, we are reminded to give thanks in all circumstances, for this aligns with God's will for us.

Cultivating gratitude in your marriage involves a deliberate and continuous effort to appreciate and value each other. It is about acknowledging the little gestures, the moments of love and support, and the unique qualities that make your spouse special.

When we express gratitude and appreciation regularly, we create an atmosphere of love and affirmation, nurturing a deeper connection and understanding in our relationship.

Reflection:

Take time to reflect on the many things you appreciate about your spouse. Consider their character traits, their acts of kindness, and the ways they have positively impacted your life.

Share your reflections with each other regularly. Take turns expressing your gratitude and appreciation for specific things your spouse has done or said. Be specific and detailed in your expressions, as this helps your spouse understand the depth of your appreciation.

Incorporate gratitude into your daily conversations, ensuring that it becomes a natural part of your interactions. a simple "thank you" for the efforts your spouse makes, no matter how small, can go a long way in affirming their value and encouraging their continued love and support.

For Her

Spiritual Practice:

Make gratitude a part of your spiritual practice as a couple. Dedicate time each day to pray together, thanking God for your spouse and your marriage.

Begin your prayer by expressing gratitude for each other and the blessings you share. Thank God for the gift of your spouse and the unique qualities they bring into your life.

Reflect on the ways your spouse has impacted your faith journey and helped you grow spiritually. Thank God for the opportunities for growth that your marriage provides.

PRAYER:

Heavenly Father,

We come before you today with hearts full of gratitude for the gift of our marriage and for the blessing of our spouse. We thank you for bringing us together and for the love that binds us.

Lord, help us to cultivate a spirit of gratitude in our marriage. Teach us to see the beauty in the small things, the love in the everyday gestures, and the joy in the moments we share together.

Thank you for the unique qualities of our spouse, for their kindness, their wisdom, and their love. We appreciate the ways they support and encourage us, and the way they bring out the best in us.

Father, we are grateful for the growth and transformation that our marriage brings. We thank you for the challenges that strengthen us and the joys that fill our hearts.

Help us to express our gratitude and appreciation to each other regularly. May our words be a source of encouragement and affirmation, deepening our love and understanding.

We also thank you for the spiritual journey we share as a couple. Thank you for the ways our faith is enriched through our marriage and for the opportunities to grow in love and grace.

Above all, we thank you for your presence in our marriage. We acknowledge that it is by Your grace that we can love and support each other. May our marriage always reflect your love and goodness to the world.

In Jesus' name, we pray,

Amen.

Closing Thoughts:

Cultivating gratitude and appreciation in your marriage is a transformative practice that fosters love, connection, and joy. As you regularly share your appreciation for each other and thank God for your spouse and your marriage, you create a space filled with love, affirmation, and mutual support.

May this week be a time of deepening gratitude, where you find joy in acknowledging the blessings that your spouse brings into your life. May you experience the beauty of a marriage rooted in gratitude, and may it strengthen your bond, drawing you closer to each other and to God's heart of love.

SUPPORTING EACH OTHER'S DREAMS

Scripture: Philippians 2:4

Let each of you look not only to his own interests, but also to the interests of others.

Devotion:

In a marriage, supporting each other's dreams is a powerful demonstration of love and commitment. When we encourage and uplift our spouses in pursuit of their aspirations, we create a foundation of trust, respect, and shared purpose. Philippians 2:4 reminds us of the importance of considering the interests of our partner above our own and valuing their dreams as much as our own.

As individuals, we all have unique dreams and goals, and it is essential to recognize that our dreams can complement and enrich each other's lives. Embracing our partner's aspirations and actively supporting their pursuit allows us to grow together and create a fulfilling and harmonious marriage.

Reflection:

Take time to reflect on your individual dreams and aspirations. Engage in an open and honest conversation with your spouse, sharing your hopes for the future and the dreams you wish to pursue.

Listen attentively to your partner's dreams and desires, seeking to understand their passions and motivations fully. Ask questions that encourage them to elaborate on their vision and how it aligns with their values and purpose.

As you discuss your individual dreams, explore how you can support each other's aspirations. Identify areas where your goals intersect or can be complementary. Discuss how you can be each other's cheerleaders, offering encouragement and assistance along the way.

For Him

For Her

Marriage Activity:

Take concrete steps to support each other's dreams. Plan a day or an evening dedicated to helping your spouse take a step forward in their pursuit.

If your spouse has a particular goal, dream, or project, dedicate time and effort to assist them in accomplishing it. This could involve brainstorming ideas, helping with research, or simply being a listening ear as they talk through their plans.

If their dream is more experiential, plan an activity or outing that aligns with their interests. For instance, if your spouse dreams of starting a small business, visit a local entrepreneur who can offer insights and advice. If they aspire to travel more, plan a day trip to a nearby destination to ignite their wanderlust.

Through this activity, you demonstrate your commitment to supporting your spouse's dreams, no matter how big or small. This shared experience can deepen your connection and foster a sense of partnership in achieving your individual aspirations.

PRAYER:

Heavenly Father,

We come before you with hearts full of gratitude for the dreams and aspirations you have placed in our hearts. We thank you for bringing us together in marriage, where we can support and uplift each other in pursuit of our individual goals.

Lord, we seek your guidance as we discuss and share our dreams with each other. Help us to listen with open hearts, valuing each other's aspirations as much as our own. Teach us to be each other's greatest supporters and encouragers.

Father, we pray for the success of our spouse's endeavors. May their efforts be fruitful and their dreams come to fruition. Grant them the wisdom, courage, and resilience they need to overcome challenges and obstacles along the way.

Help us to embrace the opportunities to grow together as we pursue our dreams side by side. May our shared journey be one of unity and mutual support, drawing us closer to each other and to you.

Lord, we surrender our plans and desires to you, trusting that your will is greater than ours. May our dreams align with your purpose for our lives, bringing glory to your name.

Thank you for the gift of marriage, where we can walk hand in hand toward our aspirations, knowing that you are with us every step of the way.

In Jesus' name, we pray,

Amen.

Closing Thoughts:

Supporting each other's dreams is a beautiful and fulfilling aspect of marriage. As you embrace this practice in your relationship, remember that your dreams can be complementary and that your journey toward your aspirations can be a shared adventure.

Take time to discuss and explore each other's dreams, and actively support and encourage each other in their pursuit. Together, as you lean on God's guidance and blessing, you will find that your marriage becomes a sanctuary of support, love, and unity as you walk hand in hand toward your dreams.

QUALITY TIME

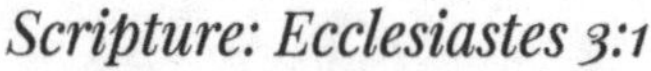
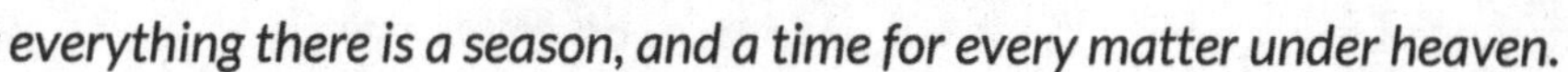

Scripture: Ecclesiastes 3:1

For everything there is a season, and a time for every matter under heaven.

Devotion:

In the fast-paced world we live in, finding time to connect with our spouse can often become a challenge. Yet, spending quality time together is essential for nurturing and strengthening the bond in our marriage. Ecclesiastes 3:1 reminds us that there is a time for everything, including setting aside precious moments to be present with our spouse.

Quality time is more than just being physically together; it is about giving each other undivided attention, fostering open communication, and creating cherished memories. When we prioritize quality time in our marriage, we build a foundation of love, trust, and intimacy that sustains us through the ups and downs of life.

Reflection:

Take time to reflect on the activities that bring joy to both you and your spouse. Engage in an open conversation about the shared experiences and moments that hold special significance in your hearts.

Discover common interests or explore new activities that you both would like to try. It could be anything from going for walks together, cooking a meal as a team, enjoying a hobby, or watching a favorite movie. The key is to find activities that enable you to connect and enjoy each other's company.

Commit to incorporating regular date nights into your routine. These intentional moments of togetherness allow you to escape the distractions of daily life and focus solely on each other. Whether you have a weekly date night or find time for a special outing once a month, these occasions become opportunities to deepen your emotional and spiritual connection.

Spiritual Practice:

Consider the spiritual practice of Lectio Divina. Begin by choosing a section of scripture that you would like to read and pray. Next, the two of you must sit in silence and prepare yourselves to hear from God. Take whatever posture will help you prepare to receive and experience God's presence.

When you both are reading, allow one of you to begin by slowly reading the passage of scripture that you have selected. Don't move quickly through any sentence or phrase. As you read, pay attention to what word, phrase, or idea catches your attention.

Pause to meditate quietly. When you are both reading, allow the other person to repeat the process of reading the passage of scripture. When you are done, what thoughts come to your mind? What are you reminded of in your life? Is God calling you to do or to be as a result of this experience?

PRAYER:

Heavenly Father,

We come before you with hearts full of gratitude for the gift of marriage and the blessing of our spouse. Thank you for the special person you have placed in our lives with whom we can share moments of love, joy, and companionship.

Lord, we recognize the importance of spending quality time together. Help us to value these moments and to be intentional in creating opportunities for togetherness.

Guide us in identifying activities that bring joy to both of us and that strengthen our emotional and spiritual bond. May our shared interests and new experiences deepen our connection and enrich our relationship.

As we commit to regular date nights, we pray for your presence in our moments of togetherness. May your love and grace fill our conversations and interactions, nurturing a spirit of love and understanding.

Lord, we ask for your blessings on our time spent together. May these moments be filled with laughter, meaningful conversations, and cherished memories. Grant us the ability to be fully present with each other, setting aside distractions and focusing on the person before us.

Help us to prioritize quality time in our marriage, knowing that this investment strengthens our love and deepens our commitment to each other.

In Jesus' name, we pray,

Amen.

Closing Thoughts:

Spending quality time together is an investment that enriches your marriage and strengthens your bond. As you prioritize these moments, remember that it is not about the grand gestures but about the genuine presence and love you offer each other.

Identify activities you both enjoy and commit to regular date nights to foster togetherness and create cherished memories. As you pray together for God's blessing on your time spent together, trust that these moments of connection will deepen your emotional and spiritual intimacy, bringing joy and fulfillment to your marriage

BUILDING FRIENDSHIPS AND COMMUNITY

Scripture: Proverbs 18:24

A man of many companions may come to ruin, but there is a friend who sticks closer than a brother.

Devotion:

In the journey of marriage, building and nurturing friendships and community connections is a valuable aspect that enriches your lives together. Proverbs 18:24 reminds us of the significance of true, meaningful friendships that provide support, understanding, and companionship.

As a couple, fostering friendships with others and engaging in a vibrant community allows you to experience shared joys and challenges, drawing strength from your connections and deepening your bond with each other.

Reflection:

This week, reflect on the friendships and community connections you currently have as a couple. Discuss the positive impact these relationships have had on your marriage and emotional well-being.

Explore opportunities to engage with other couples or communities that align with your interests and values. This could involve attending social events, joining a group or organization, or participating in activities that allow you to meet new people.

Consider the benefits of having shared friendships with other couples. These connections can offer a support system, opportunities for growth, and a sense of belonging that strengthens both your individual lives and your life together as a couple.

For Him

For Her

Marriage Activity:

Go on a double date with another married couple. During your interactions with the other couple, be intentional in listening and learning from others' experiences. Share your own journey, challenges, and triumphs, allowing for mutual support and empathy.

Embrace these moments as opportunities to grow together as a couple, strengthening your bond as you engage with others on a deeper level.

PRAYER:

Heavenly Father,

We come before you with hearts full of gratitude for the gift of friendship and community. Thank you for placing people in our lives who support and enrich us.

Lord, as a couple, we seek to build and nurture meaningful relationships with others. Guide us in connecting with other couples or communities that align with our values and aspirations.

Grant us the ability to be open and vulnerable, allowing our friendships to grow and deepen. May our interactions with others be filled with empathy, understanding, and compassion.

We pray for true friends who stick closer than brothers, individuals who support and uplift us through life's joys and challenges. Bless our relationships with trust, loyalty, and love.

As we engage with others, help us to be a source of encouragement and support. May our presence in their lives reflect your love and grace.

Father, we also pray for the strengthening of our marriage through these connections. May the friendships we build together enrich our lives and bring joy to our journey.

Above all, we seek your guidance in fostering a vibrant community that allows us to grow and thrive. May our shared connections with others deepen our bond and nurture a sense of belonging.

In Jesus' name, we pray,

Amen.

Closing Thoughts:

Building friendships and engaging in community activities is an enriching practice that strengthens your marriage and emotional well-being. Embrace the opportunity to connect with other couples and share your journey with them.

As you engage with others, remember to be open, vulnerable, and supportive. Seek God's guidance in nurturing these connections and pray for meaningful relationships that enrich your lives and bring joy to your marriage.

May this week be a time of growth, connection, and joy as you build meaningful friendships and embrace the beauty of community connections together as a couple.

SETTING BOUNDARIES

Scripture: Proverbs 4:23

Keep your heart with all vigilance, for from it flow the springs of life.

Devotion:

In every successful and thriving marriage, the establishment of healthy boundaries is essential. Proverbs 4:23 reminds us to guard our hearts diligently, as everything we do flows from the state of our hearts.

Boundaries in marriage are guidelines that protect the emotional, physical, and spiritual well-being of both partners. They create a safe space for open communication, individual growth, and mutual respect.

Establishing and maintaining boundaries is a sign of love and respect for each other's needs and desires. By setting boundaries, we create an environment where both partners can feel secure and supported, fostering a stronger and more intimate connection.

Reflection:

Take time as a couple to reflect on your individual needs and personal boundaries. Engage in an open and honest conversation about what makes you feel comfortable and respected in various aspects of your marriage.

Discuss your emotional, physical, and spiritual boundaries. Be honest about any areas where you feel your boundaries are being challenged or crossed, and listen attentively to your partner's concerns.

In this conversation, focus on understanding each other's perspectives without judgment. The goal is to create an environment where both partners feel heard, valued, and validated in their desires and limitations.

FOR HER

Spiritual Practice:

Make prayer a central part of your commitment to setting and respecting boundaries in your marriage. Dedicate time each day to pray together, asking for God's guidance and wisdom in this process.

Pray for the ability to communicate openly and honestly with each other, showing understanding and empathy as you discuss boundaries. Ask God to help you both prioritize each other's emotional and spiritual well-being in setting these guidelines.

Seek God's grace to respect and honor each other's boundaries with love and compassion. Pray for strength and patience to uphold the boundaries you have set, knowing that they contribute to a healthier and more fulfilling marriage.

PRAYER:

Heavenly Father,

We come before you with hearts open to your guidance and wisdom. Thank you for the gift of marriage, where we can learn to love and respect each other unconditionally.

Lord, as we seek to set boundaries in our marriage, we ask for your wisdom and understanding. Help us to communicate openly and honestly, showing empathy and compassion as we discuss our individual needs and desires.

Grant us the ability to prioritize each other's emotional and spiritual well-being, acknowledging that healthy boundaries contribute to a stronger and more intimate connection.

We pray for the strength and grace to uphold the boundaries we have set, knowing that they create a safe and supportive environment for our love to grow.

Father, we ask for your guidance in respecting each other's boundaries with love and understanding. May our actions and words always be aligned with the mutual respect and love we have for one another.

Above all, we seek to guard our hearts diligently, as everything we do flows from the state of our hearts. May our boundaries be a reflection of your love and grace in our marriage.

In Jesus' name, we pray,

Amen.

Closing Thoughts:

Establishing healthy boundaries is an essential aspect of a thriving and fulfilling marriage. As you set boundaries together, remember to communicate openly, show empathy, and prioritize each other's well-being.

Prayer plays a vital role in this process, as it allows you to seek God's guidance and wisdom in respecting and upholding these guidelines. May this week be a time of growth, understanding, and deeper intimacy as you establish healthy boundaries that strengthen your bond and nurture a love that flows from the heart.

ACTS OF SERVICE

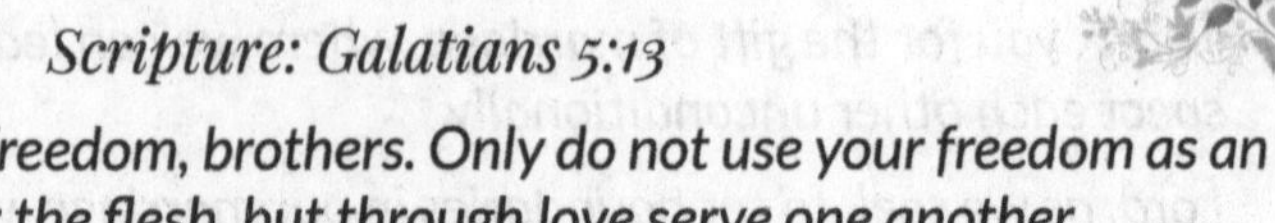

Scripture: Galatians 5:13

For you were called to freedom, brothers. Only do not use your freedom as an opportunity for the flesh, but through love serve one another.

Devotion:

In the journey of marriage, acts of service are a powerful expression of love and care. Galatians 5:13 reminds us of the call to serve one another humbly in love, recognizing that true freedom comes from selfless actions that enrich our relationships.

Acts of service go beyond mere gestures; they are heartfelt expressions of love that demonstrate our willingness to prioritize our partner's well-being above our own. By serving each other with love, we create an environment of compassion, support, and mutual respect in our marriage.

Reflection:

Take time as a couple to reflect on the various ways you can serve each other and demonstrate love through acts of service. Discuss the tasks, responsibilities, and gestures that would make a significant difference in each other's lives.

Identify both small and meaningful acts of service that would bring joy and relief to your partner. It could be as simple as preparing breakfast in bed, helping with household chores, or offering a listening ear after a long day.

Emphasize the importance of serving with a heart full of love and humility. Genuine acts of service are not performed out of obligation but with a deep desire to see your partner happy and cared for.

Marriage Activity:

Create a list of acts of service that you both commit to performing for each other throughout the week. Consider this list as a tangible expression of your love and care for one another.

Take turns serving each other, ensuring that these acts of service are performed with intentionality and love. Focus on the joy of giving and the joy of receiving, knowing that both roles are equally significant in nurturing your bond.

PRAYER:

Heavenly Father,

We come before you with hearts open to your love and guidance. Thank you for the gift of marriage, where we can learn to serve and love one another with humility.

Lord, as we commit to acts of service in our marriage, we pray for a servant's heart that mirrors your love for us. Teach us to serve each other selflessly, finding joy in giving and caring for each other's needs.

May our acts of service be expressions of love and compassion, creating a safe and supportive space for our partner to thrive.

Grant us the wisdom to discern the needs of our spouse and the strength to serve them even when it requires sacrifice. May our love be a reflection of your love, selfless and unwavering.

Lord, we ask for your blessings on our acts of service, knowing that they strengthen our bond and deepen our connection.

Above all, help us to serve with love and humility, recognizing that true freedom comes from selfless actions that enrich our relationships.

In Jesus' name, we pray,

Amen.

Closing Thoughts:

Acts of service are a beautiful and transformative expression of love in a marriage. As you commit to serving each other with humility and love, remember that genuine acts of service are not merely tasks but heartfelt gestures that prioritize your partner's well-being.

May this week be a time of growth, understanding, and deeper intimacy as you embrace a servant's heart in your marriage. May your acts of service create a bond of love and compassion that reflects God's love for you both, nurturing a relationship that thrives in selflessness and care.

PARENTING TOGETHER

Scripture: Psalm 127:3

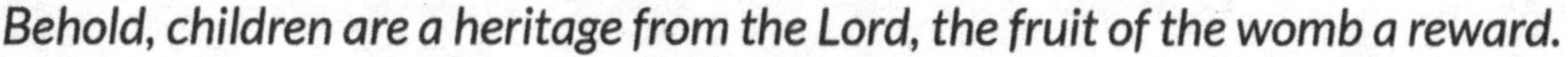

Behold, children are a heritage from the Lord, the fruit of the womb a reward.

Devotion:

Parenthood is a sacred and transformative journey, and Psalm 127:3 beautifully captures the significance of children in our lives. As parents, we are entrusted with the precious gift of raising the next generation, guiding them with love and wisdom. Embracing this journey as a team is crucial for the well-being of both our children and our marriage.

Parenting together as a united team strengthens your bond as a couple and provides a stable and nurturing environment for your children to thrive. When both partners actively participate in the joys and challenges of parenting, it fosters a sense of partnership and shared responsibility.

Reflection:

Set aside time to have an open and honest conversation about your parenting journey. Reflect on your parenting roles and responsibilities, and discuss how you can support each other in your individual tasks.

Identify your core parenting values and beliefs, and explore how they align with each other. Discuss any differences in your approaches to parenting, and seek common ground that will allow you to provide a consistent and loving environment for your children.

Explore disciplinary approaches that you both find effective and fair. Consider how you can present a united front to your children, offering guidance and discipline with love and understanding.

Spiritual Practice:

Parenting requires patience, and patience is part of the Fruit of the Spirit. This week, we will begin to pray for patience and understanding as you navigate the challenges of parenthood or even future parenthood.

At the same time, begin by identifying when you're impatient and what emotion you are feeling. Then, reframe how you think about the situation. Try putting yourself in the other person's shoes and think with purpose in mind.

For example, if your toddler is pouting because she is being served green beans instead of ice cream, remember that it is more important that she learns what healthy eating means and gets into a routine of eating that way.

As you put this spiritual practice into motion, you will better understand the people around you and become more patient.

PRAYER:

Heavenly Father,

We come before you with grateful hearts for the precious gift of our children. Thank you for entrusting us with the responsibility of raising them and guiding them in your love.

Lord, as we embark on this journey of parenthood together, we pray for unity and strength as a team. May our love for each other and for our children deepen and grow.

We seek your wisdom in defining our parenting roles, values, and disciplinary approaches. Help us to support and uplift each other in our individual tasks, recognizing that together, we create a nurturing environment for our children to flourish.

Lord, grant us the ability to lead by example, instilling in our children the values that align with your will. May they grow to be compassionate, kind, and responsible individuals who reflect your love in their lives.

As we encounter challenges and triumphs in our parenting journey, we pray for your guidance and grace. Help us to communicate with love and understanding, fostering a strong and loving bond with our children.

Above all, we seek your wisdom in making important decisions about our children's upbringing and well-being. May your wisdom guide us in providing the love and guidance they need to grow into their full potential.

In Jesus' name, we pray,

Amen.

Closing Thoughts:

Parenting together as a team is a beautiful and transformative experience. As you embrace the journey of parenthood united, remember to discuss your parenting roles, values, and disciplinary approaches.

Create a parenting plan that outlines your responsibilities and shared values as parents, and seek God's guidance through prayer as you raise your children with love and guidance.

May this week be a time of growth, understanding, and deeper connection as you navigate parenthood together as a team, nurturing your children with love and wisdom to become blessings in their own right.

NAVIGATING LIFE TRANSITIONS

Scripture: Ecclesiastes 3:4

A time to weep, and a time to laugh; a time to mourn, and a time to dance.

Devotion:

Life is a tapestry woven with threads of diverse experiences, and Ecclesiastes 3:4 eloquently reminds us of the ebb and flow of life's seasons. Within this poetic verse lies a profound truth: Life is composed of moments that are both joyful and challenging, and it is in navigating these transitions together that our strength and unity as a couple are truly tested and revealed.

Transitions, whether they herald moments of celebration or moments of difficulty, are an integral part of the human journey. As you navigate these changing seasons side by side, your partnership deepens, and your capacity to lean on each other for support and encouragement becomes even more essential.

Reflection:

This week, reflect on any impending life transitions that you as a couple are preparing to navigate. These transitions could encompass a range of experiences, such as embarking on a new chapter in your career, relocating to a different place, or welcoming a new member into your family.

Create a sacred space for open and heartfelt conversation. Share your individual fears and hopes regarding these upcoming changes, acknowledging the mix of emotions that arise during times of transition. Listen attentively to your partner's thoughts and feelings, offering empathy and understanding.

By creating an atmosphere of mutual support, you reinforce the strength of your partnership. Remember that, as a team, you have the power to turn moments of uncertainty into opportunities for growth and transformation.

For Her

Marriage Activity:

Embark on an activity that symbolizes your shared journey through life's transitions. It could be as simple as taking a walk together through nature, where you can witness the changing seasons and reflect on the beauty of transformation.

As you walk, discuss the specific transition you are currently navigating and the ways in which you can provide emotional support for one another. Share your strategies for coping with change, and commit to walking through these seasons hand in hand.

PRAYER:

Heavenly Father,

As we stand on the threshold of change, we come before you, seeking your guidance and strength. Your wisdom is our compass, and your love is our anchor.

Lord, we recognize that life is a series of transitions—moments of both sorrow and joy, growth and challenge. Grant us the grace to lean on each other during these times, finding strength and unity as we journey through change together.

In the face of uncertainty, we bring our fears and hopes before you. We lay our worries at your feet and place our trust in your unwavering care.

As we walk through life's seasons, may our steps be guided by your light. Illuminate our path so that we may discern the lessons, purpose, and blessings within each transition.

Father, may our partnership be a testament to your love and grace. Help us to support and uplift one another, finding solace in the embrace of a shared journey.

In moments of laughter and moments of tears, may our hearts be steadfast in your love. May our unity be an instrument of your peace, and may we dance through life's changes with hearts full of gratitude.

In Jesus' name, we pray,

Amen.

Closing Thoughts:

Life's transitions are an integral part of our journey, and our response to them as a couple can deepen our bond and strengthen our faith. By sharing your fears and hopes, and seeking God's guidance through prayer, you can navigate these changes with unity and grace.

Embrace the beauty of transformation and find solace in the knowledge that, like the changing seasons, every moment has its purpose. May this week be a time of deepening connection, mutual support, and unwavering trust as you navigate life's transitions together, dancing through change hand in hand.

KEEPING THE ROMANCE ALIVE

Scripture: Song of Solomon 1:2

Let him kiss me with the kisses of his mouth! For your love is better than wine.

Devotion:

Romance is the vibrant thread that weaves through the fabric of a loving marriage. Song of Solomon 1:2 captures the essence of longing and desire, reminding us of the intoxicating power of love. As time passes, the flames of passion may flicker, but they need not fade. Embracing the call to keep the romance alive infuses new energy and vitality into your relationship.

Romance is more than a fleeting emotion; it's a deliberate choice to nurture and express love in creative and affectionate ways. Reigniting passion involves kindling the sparks that first brought you together, reminding each other of the captivating allure that continues to exist.

Reflection:

This week, engage in an open and candid discussion about how you can infuse your marriage with ongoing acts of love and affection. Reflect on the gestures and experiences that once made your hearts flutter and explore how to incorporate them into your current lives.

Share your desires and aspirations for the romantic aspect of your marriage. Discuss your love languages and how you can use them to communicate love and care effectively. Emphasize the importance of consistent effort in keeping the flame of romance alive.

Spiritual Practice:

We need to be mindful that spiritual practices include anything that opens our attention to the presence of God. Throughout this devotional, you will notice that each spiritual practice typically involves meditation or scripture reading; however, a spiritual practice can be as simple as watching the sunset or even intimacy between a man and a woman.

Within this moment, we can discover that there is more than just meeting a physical or emotional need. Two people can begin to reflect His divine love within the holy freedom found within marriage. The act of love becomes a deeper, more spiritual experience if we keep our awareness of God's presence in the moment.

This, of course, may seem weird or, in some cases, wrong at first; however, the spiritual practice of intimacy will bring greater fulfillment and joy. Remembering that God created this type of intimacy, and when it is done within the confines of marriage, it is a beautiful moment.

PRAYER:

Heavenly Father,

We come before you with hearts open to your guidance and grace. Thank you for the gift of love and romance in our marriage, a reflection of your boundless love for us.

Lord, as we seek to keep the flame of romance alive, we ask for your wisdom and inspiration. Help us to express our love and affection in ways that touch each other's hearts deeply.

May our actions and words be a testament to the love that flows between us. Rekindle the passion that first brought us together, reminding us of the beauty and allure that continue to exist.

We pray for a deeper, more intimate connection in our marriage. May our physical and emotional bond be nurtured by your presence and grace.

Father, bless our romantic journey. May our efforts to keep the romance alive be a source of joy and strength, enhancing our love for one another.

In Jesus' name, we pray,

Amen.

Closing Thoughts:

Romance is an essential ingredient that keeps the heart of a marriage beating strongly. By intentionally nurturing the romantic aspect of your relationship, you can reignite the passion and deepen the connection between you and your partner.

Through open conversations, shared experiences, and heartfelt prayers, you can infuse your marriage with the warmth and tenderness that initially brought you together. May this week be a time of renewed passion, deep connection, and rekindled romance as you commit to keeping the flame alive in your marriage, guided by the wisdom of God's love.

FOSTERING GRATITUDE AND CONTENTMENT

Scripture: Philippians 4:11

Not that I am speaking of being in need, for I have learned in whatever situation I am to be content.

Devotion:

In a world often marked by the pursuit of more, Philippians 4:11 serves as a gentle reminder of the power of contentment. It speaks of finding peace and satisfaction, not in external circumstances, but in the deep wellspring of our hearts. Cultivating a heart of gratitude and contentment in marriage transforms our perspective and enriches our bond.

Contentment is not complacency; rather, it is a choice to appreciate and find joy in the present moment, recognizing that true abundance is found in the love and connection we share. When we foster gratitude, we discover the beauty of simple blessings and the richness of the life we have built together.

Reflection:

This week, embark on a journey of reflection and appreciation. Take time to count your blessings, both as individuals and as a couple. Reflect on the moments of joy, growth, and connection that have woven the tapestry of your relationship.

Create a list of things you are grateful for in each other. Express your gratitude for the qualities, gestures, and actions that make your partner unique and cherished. Sharing these expressions of gratitude fosters a culture of appreciation in your marriage.

For Her

Marriage Activity:

As a marriage activity, engage in a "gratitude exchange." Each day, take turns sharing something you are grateful for about your partner. It could be a specific act of kindness, a character trait you admire, or a shared experience that has enriched your connection.

Embrace the opportunity to listen and receive, allowing the expressions of gratitude to deepen your understanding of each other's hearts. Create a space of warmth and appreciation that strengthens the foundation of your relationship.

PRAYER:

Heavenly Father,

We come before you with hearts full of gratitude for the love and blessings you have bestowed upon us. Thank you for the gift of each other and the journey of marriage.

Lord, as we seek to foster gratitude and contentment in our marriage, we ask for your guidance and presence. Teach us to find joy in the present moment and to appreciate the simple blessings that surround us.

Help us to learn from the example of the apostle Paul, who found contentment in every situation. May our hearts be steadfast, rooted in the love we share and the connection we have built.

Father, as we count our blessings and express gratitude toward one another, may our relationship deepen and flourish. Create a spirit of appreciation that strengthens our bond and enriches our lives.

We pray for the grace to find contentment amidst challenges and to recognize the beauty that exists in our relationship. Open our eyes to the abundance of love, connection, and shared experiences that fill our days.

In moments of restlessness, help us remember that true fulfillment comes from you. Guide us to find contentment not in the pursuit of more but in the depth of the love we nurture.

In Jesus' name, we pray,

Amen.

Closing Thoughts:

Fostering gratitude and contentment is a transformative practice that elevates your marriage to new heights of appreciation and joy. By focusing on the blessings, you share and cultivating a heart of contentment, you deepen your connection and enrich your lives.

Through reflection, expressions of gratitude, and heartfelt prayers, you invite God's presence into your pursuit of contentment, recognizing that true fulfillment is found in the love you nurture together. May this week be a time of deepened gratitude, strengthened bond, and enriched perspective as you commit to fostering gratitude and contentment in your marriage.

SUPPORTING EACH OTHER'S SPIRITUAL GROWTH

Scripture: Proverbs 27:17

Iron sharpens iron, and one man sharpens another.

Devotion:

Marriage is a union that extends beyond the earthly realm, encompassing the spiritual dimension of our lives. Proverbs 27:17 beautifully illustrates the concept of mutual growth and influence, comparing it to the way iron sharpens iron. Just as two pieces of metal refine each other's edges, so too can spouses nurture and uplift each other's spiritual journeys.

Supporting each other's spiritual growth is a profound and sacred responsibility. As you encourage and uplift one another, your connection deepens, and your shared journey becomes a path of transformation and enlightenment.

Reflection:

This week, embark on a journey of shared spiritual reflection. Take time to explore and discuss your individual spiritual goals, aspirations, and desires. Create a safe space to share your personal experiences with faith and your aspirations for deepening your spiritual connection.

In this dialogue, listen with an open heart and offer unwavering support to your partner's spiritual journey. Reflect on the ways in which you can contribute to each other's growth, drawing strength from the beautiful bond you share.

For Him

For Her

Spiritual Practice:

Spiritual journeys can feel like solo journeys, but they don't have to be. Some of the best experiences happen in our interconnectedness with our partner. We are individuals, not islands. We are social beings, and we are also spiritual ones.

Now might be a good time to start a couple's spiritual journal. Allow it to be a safe space where one can organize their thoughts by sitting down with a pen and paper. Set a timer for 5, 10, or maybe even 15 minutes, and don't stop writing until the timer goes off. Write about what you are feeling, especially positive ones, then step back and discover something new about yourself or even your partner.

PRAYER:

Heavenly Father,

We come before you as a couple seeking to strengthen our spiritual journeys. Thank you for the gift of faith and the opportunity to walk this path of growth and enlightenment together.

Lord, as we support each other's spiritual growth, we ask for your guidance and grace. Help us to be attuned to one another's needs and aspirations, encouraging each other along the way.

We pray for the wisdom to recognize the intersections in our spiritual journeys. May our bond serve as a source of strength and inspiration as we navigate the twists and turns of this path.

Father, we lift up our individual spiritual goals to you. Grant us the perseverance to pursue them with dedication and humility. May our pursuits draw us closer to you and to each other.

As we engage in shared spiritual practices, may our hearts be open to your presence. Help us to learn from each other's insights and experiences, enriching our own understanding of faith.

In moments of doubt or uncertainty, remind us of the wisdom found in your word. Like iron sharpening iron, may our partnership refine and uplift our souls, bringing us closer to your divine light.

In Jesus' name, we pray,

Amen.

Closing Thoughts:

Supporting each other's spiritual growth is a profound expression of love and partnership. By sharing individual spiritual goals, engaging in joint practices, and inviting God's presence through prayer, you create a sacred space for mutual upliftment and transformation.

As you journey together on the path of faith, may your partnership serve as a source of strength, wisdom, and inspiration. Through your commitment to supporting each other's spiritual growth, you deepen your bond and nurture a connection that transcends the ordinary, enriching your lives with divine purpose and meaning.

OVERCOMING CHALLENGES TOGETHER

Scripture: 1 Peter 4:12

Beloved, do not be surprised at the fiery trial when it comes upon you to test you, as though something strange were happening to you.

Devotion:

Challenges are an inevitable part of life's journey, and 1 Peter 4:12 reminds us that trials are not something strange or unexpected. In fact, they serve as opportunities for growth, transformation, and the strengthening of our character. As a couple, facing challenges together can deepen your bond and fortify your partnership with resilience.

Building resilience in the face of challenges involves a shift in perspective. Rather than viewing difficulties as insurmountable obstacles, you can embrace them as stepping stones toward a stronger and more united marriage.

Reflection:

Take time this week to reflect on the challenges you and your partner have encountered and overcome together. Celebrate the victories you have achieved as a team, acknowledging the strength and determination that have carried you through difficult times.

Discuss the ways in which these challenges have shaped your relationship. Reflect on the lessons learned, the growth you have experienced, and the ways in which adversity has brought you closer together.

Marriage Activity:

As a marriage activity, embark on a joint project that symbolizes your ability to overcome challenges as a united front. It could be a home improvement task, a creative endeavor, or even a physical challenge, such as hiking to a scenic spot.

During this activity, work together to achieve a specific goal. Embrace the process as a metaphor for overcoming challenges in your marriage, focusing on communication, cooperation, and shared determination.

PRAYER:

Heavenly Father,

We come before you as a couple, united in the face of challenges. Thank you for the strength and resilience you have bestowed upon us.

Lord, as we encounter trials on our journey, help us to remember that challenges are not strange or unexpected. Teach us to view them as opportunities for growth and transformation, knowing that you are with us every step of the way.

We celebrate the victories we have achieved together in the past. Thank you for the lessons learned and the growth experienced through these challenges. May our shared experiences continue to shape and strengthen our bond.

As we engage in our marriage activity, may it serve as a reminder of our ability to overcome obstacles as a team. Guide us to work together with patience, understanding, and cooperation.

Father, we seek your strength to face challenges with resilience and faith. In moments of doubt, may we find reassurance in your presence. In moments of difficulty, may we draw on your wisdom to find solutions.

We pray for your grace to sustain us as we navigate the trials of life. May our partnership be a testament to your love and our commitment to each other.

In Jesus' name, we pray,

Amen.

Closing Thoughts:

Overcoming challenges together is a testament to the strength and unity of your marriage. By reflecting on past victories, engaging in joint activities, and inviting God's strength through prayer, you fortify your bond and cultivate resilience in the face of adversity.

As you journey through life's trials, may your partnership be a source of inspiration and support. Embrace challenges as opportunities for growth, knowing that you are united by love and guided by faith. Through your commitment to facing challenges together, you build a foundation of strength and unity that can weather any storm.

CULTIVATING PATIENCE AND KINDNESS

Scripture: 1 Corinthians 13:4a
Love is patient and kind.

Devotion:

1 Corinthians 13:4a beautifully captures two essential qualities of love: patience and kindness. These attributes are like the gentle rain and warm sunshine that nourish the soil of marriage, allowing it to thrive and flourish. Cultivating patience and kindness in your relationship is a powerful expression of love that brings harmony, understanding, and lasting joy.

Patience is the art of waiting with grace, of extending understanding when challenges arise. Kindness is the language of love spoken through actions and words that uplift and affirm. Together, these qualities create a foundation of compassion that transforms ordinary moments into extraordinary connections.

Reflection:

This week, engage in a heartfelt conversation with your partner about the practice of patience and kindness within your marriage. Reflect on moments when these qualities have enriched your relationship, and also explore areas where there is room for improvement.

Create a safe space for open dialogue. Share your thoughts and feelings about instances when patience or kindness may have been lacking, and listen attentively to your partner's perspective. Approach this reflection with humility and a shared commitment to growth.

Spiritual Practice:

Integrate prayer into your commitment to cultivating patience and kindness. Dedicate time each day to pray together, inviting God's presence to guide your hearts toward greater understanding, patience, and kindness.

Pray for the wisdom to respond to each other with patience, even in moments of tension. Ask for the ability to extend kindness through your words and actions, nurturing a spirit of empathy and compassion.

Seek God's help to overcome challenges that may test your patience and kindness. Pray for the strength to choose love and understanding in all circumstances, knowing that these qualities reflect His divine nature.

PRAYER:

Heavenly Father,

We come before you as a couple seeking to deepen our love through patience and kindness. Thank you for the gift of love that is patient and kind, reflecting your own nature.

Lord, as we strive to embody these qualities in our marriage, we ask for your guidance and strength. Help us to wait with grace and extend understanding when challenges arise.

Teach us the language of kindness, that our words and actions may uplift and affirm. May our interactions be marked by a spirit of empathy and compassion.

In our reflection, we recognize moments when patience and kindness have enriched our relationship. We also acknowledge areas where we can improve. Grant us the humility to learn and grow together.

As we engage in intentional acts of kindness, may our actions speak love louder than words. Strengthen our bond through these gestures, reminding us of the beauty that emerges when we choose kindness.

Father, in moments of frustration or impatience, remind us of your love. In times of tension, guide us to respond with patience and understanding. May our marriage be a testament to your transformative power.

In Jesus' name, we pray,

Amen.

Closing Thoughts:

Cultivating patience and kindness in your marriage is a transformative practice that nurtures love, understanding, and connection. By reflecting on these qualities, engaging in acts of kindness, and seeking God's guidance through prayer, you create a foundation of compassion that strengthens your bond.

Through your commitment to patience and kindness, you choose to respond to each other with grace and understanding, even in the midst of challenges. May this week be a time of deepened empathy, strengthened love, and enduring joy as you cultivate the beautiful qualities of patience and kindness within your marriage.

BUILDING TRUST
AFTER BETRAYAL

Scripture: Proverbs 3:5
Trust in the Lord with all your heart, and do not lean on your own
understanding.

Devotion:

Betrayal within a marriage is a deeply painful experience that challenges the very foundation of trust. Yet, even in the face of such adversity, the wisdom of Proverbs 3:5 offers a guiding light. Trusting in the Lord with all your heart becomes the anchor that holds you steady as you navigate the difficult journey of healing and rebuilding trust.

The path to restoring trust after betrayal is a delicate one, paved with open communication, vulnerability, and a shared commitment to transformation. It's an opportunity for both partners to lean on God's understanding and guidance as they work toward rebuilding what was broken.

Reflection:

This week, create a space of authenticity and vulnerability as you engage in a heart-to-heart conversation about the breach of trust that occurred. Both partners should share their feelings, fears, and hopes regarding the betrayal and its impact on the relationship.

Listen attentively to each other's perspectives without judgment. Allow this reflection to foster understanding and empathy, providing a foundation for the challenging but necessary journey ahead.

For Him

For Her

Marriage Activity:

As a marriage activity, engage in a joint exercise aimed at rebuilding trust. This could involve creating a "Trust Building Plan" together, outlining specific actions and behaviors that will contribute to rebuilding trust over time.

Commit to the plan as a sign of your shared dedication to healing and transformation. This activity serves as a tangible manifestation of your mutual commitment to rebuilding trust.

PRAYER:

Heavenly Father,

We come before you with heavy hearts, seeking your guidance and strength as we navigate the challenging path of rebuilding trust after betrayal.

Lord, we acknowledge the pain and hurt that has been caused. As we reflect on this breach of trust, help us to communicate our feelings, fears, and hopes openly and honestly.

Grant us the wisdom to understand each other's perspectives, even when the road ahead seems uncertain. May our shared vulnerability foster empathy and compassion.

As we engage in the marriage activity to rebuild trust, we recognize the significance of our commitment. Guide us in creating a plan that reflects our shared dedication to healing and transformation.

Father, we invite you into our journey of restoration. We pray for the strength to forgive and the humility to seek forgiveness. Heal our wounded hearts and grant us the grace to move forward together.

In moments of doubt and uncertainty, remind us to trust in you with all our hearts. As we lean on your understanding, may we find the courage to face the challenges before us.

We seek your guidance, Lord, knowing that through your presence, all things are possible. May our efforts to rebuild trust be guided by your wisdom and love.

In Jesus' name, we pray,

Amen.

Closing Thoughts:

Rebuilding trust after betrayal is a courageous and transformative journey that requires vulnerability, understanding, and a shared commitment to healing. By leaning on God's understanding, engaging in open communication, and seeking His guidance through prayer, you pave the way for restoration and renewal.

Through your dedication to healing and rebuilding trust, you not only mend what was broken but also strengthen your bond with a newfound depth of understanding and empathy. May this week be a time of healing, growth, and renewed hope as you embrace the journey of rebuilding trust with faith and love.

EMBRACING EACH OTHER'S DIFFERENCES

Scripture: Romans 12:5

So we, though many, are one body in Christ, and individually members one of another.

Devotion:

In the tapestry of marriage, each partner brings a unique thread of identity, perspective, and experience. Romans 12:5 reminds us that although we are many, we are intricately woven together as one body. Just as the diverse parts of the body work together in harmony, so too do the distinct qualities of each spouse contribute to the beauty and strength of the marital union. Embracing each other's differences is an essential practice that fosters unity, understanding, and growth. It's an invitation to celebrate the richness that diversity brings to your relationship and to honor the unique qualities that make each partner a precious and irreplaceable part of the whole.

Reflection:

This week, engage in a thoughtful and open conversation about the unique qualities, strengths, and perspectives that each partner brings to the marriage. Reflect on how these differences complement and challenge each other, enriching the fabric of your relationship.

Explore how your diverse qualities have contributed to your growth as individuals and as a couple. Acknowledge the moments when your differences have provided new insights and alternative viewpoints, expanding your understanding of the world and each other.

FOR HER

Spiritual Practice:

Learning to be flexible and supportive on your spiritual journey is important. By now, you have gone through a few spiritual practices together, and now it's time to discuss your favorites. What brought you closer to God? Was there a spiritual practice you didn't care for, and why?

Take turns practicing each other's favorite spiritual practice. Discover what made it your partner's favorite. Try to learn about how each other connects with God and embrace each other's differences.

PRAYER:

Heavenly Father,

We come before you as a couple, grateful for the diverse qualities that make us who we are. Thank you for creating us as unique individuals, each with our own perspectives, strengths, and experiences.

Lord, as we seek to embrace each other's differences, we ask for your guidance and understanding. Help us to recognize the value of these differences, understanding that they enrich our relationship and contribute to our growth.

As we reflect on how our qualities complement and challenge each other, may our hearts be open to new insights and deeper understanding. Grant us the wisdom to appreciate the perspectives that each partner brings to the marriage.

In our joint creative activity, we celebrate the beauty that emerges when our differences are integrated. Guide our hands and hearts as we work together, symbolizing the unity that comes from embracing diversity.

Father, we seek your presence in moments when challenges arise due to our differences. May your spirit of patience and compromise prevail, allowing us to navigate these instances with grace and love.

We pray for the grace to see each other as you see us—precious and uniquely crafted. Strengthen our bond as we commit to embracing each other's differences with understanding and appreciation.

In Jesus' name, we pray,

Amen.

Closing Thoughts:

Embracing each other's differences is a powerful practice that deepens your understanding, appreciation, and connection. By reflecting on your unique qualities, engaging in joint creative activities, and seeking God's guidance through prayer, you cultivate a spirit of unity that transcends individuality.

Through your commitment to embracing differences, you honor the intricate tapestry of your marriage and recognize the divine wisdom that brought you together. May this week be a time of deepened appreciation, enriched perspective, and renewed unity as you celebrate and embrace each other's unique qualities with love and gratitude.

RESOLVING FAMILY CONFLICTS

Scripture: Ephesians 4:31

Let all bitterness and wrath and anger and clamor and slander be put away from you, along with all malice.

Devotion:

In the tapestry of marriage, the threads of extended family relationships are intricately woven. These connections can bring both joy and challenge, and Ephesians 4:31 offers valuable guidance for navigating conflicts within this complex web of relationships.

When conflicts arise with extended family members, it's an opportunity to practice the virtues of forgiveness, understanding, and unity. The command to put away bitterness, wrath, anger, and malice underscores the importance of maintaining a spirit of love and grace even in the face of disagreements.

Reflection:

This week, engage in a reflective conversation with your partner about the challenges that may arise from conflicts with extended family members. Explore specific situations that have caused tension or discord, and discuss your feelings, concerns, and hopes for maintaining unity.

Together, establish healthy boundaries that protect your marriage while still honoring your extended family relationships. Reflect on how you can communicate these boundaries respectfully and effectively to avoid further conflict.

Marriage Activity:

As a marriage activity, collaborate on a written agreement or plan for addressing family conflicts. This plan could outline strategies for open communication, boundary-setting, and approaching conflicts with a spirit of understanding and empathy.

By creating a unified approach, you reinforce your commitment to handling family conflicts as a team and ensure that both partners are on the same page when navigating these challenges.

PRAYER:

Heavenly Father,

As a couple, we come before you with open hearts, seeking your guidance and wisdom in navigating conflicts with our extended family members.

Lord, we acknowledge the challenges that can arise from these relationships. As we reflect on Ephesians 4:31, we recognize the importance of putting away bitterness, anger, and malice.

Grant us the strength to respond with love and understanding, even in moments of tension. Help us to establish healthy boundaries that protect our marriage while still honoring our family connections.

As we create a plan for addressing family conflicts, guide us in forming a unified approach. May our commitment to resolving conflicts as a team strengthen our bond and lead to greater unity.

Father, we invite your presence into the midst of family tensions. Fill our hearts with your peace, and grant us the humility to seek reconciliation and understanding.

In moments of disagreement, remind us of your command to love one another. May our interactions be marked by a spirit of grace and empathy.

We pray for your wisdom in knowing when to speak and when to listen. May your guidance lead us toward resolutions that promote understanding and harmony.

In Jesus' name, we pray,

Amen.

Closing Thoughts:

Resolving family conflicts is a delicate yet essential practice that strengthens your marriage and fosters unity. By reflecting on Ephesians 4:31, creating a plan for addressing conflicts, and seeking God's guidance through prayer, you navigate the complex landscape of extended family relationships with grace and understanding.

Through your commitment to handling conflicts with love and wisdom, you honor both your marriage and your family connections. May this week be a time of growth, unity, and renewed understanding as you navigate family tensions with humility and a shared dedication to reconciliation.

BUILDING A STRONG SUPPORT SYSTEM

Scripture: Ecclesiastes 4:9

Two are better than one because they have a good reward for their toil.

Devotion:

Marriage is a journey that is meant to be shared, a path where two souls come together to navigate life's joys and challenges as a united team. Ecclesiastes 4:9 reminds us of the inherent strength that comes from companionship—the power of two working in harmony to achieve a greater reward for their efforts.

Yet, a strong marriage is not built in isolation. Just as a tree needs a firm foundation and nurturing soil to grow tall and strong, a marriage thrives when surrounded by a strong support system. This support system, composed of friends, mentors, and like-minded couples, provides a nurturing environment where your love can take root, grow, and flourish.

Reflection:

This week, take time to reflect on the importance of building a robust support system for your marriage. Consider the friends and mentors who have positively influenced your relationship and contributed to your growth as a couple.

Reflect on the qualities that make these relationships meaningful and how they have enriched your journey. Identify the individuals who uplift, encourage, and provide wisdom that aligns with your marriage values.

Spiritual Practice:

Incorporate a Spiritual Director or a pastor into your spiritual journey together. Someone who will ask the tough questions that you might not be thinking of. The most important thing to keep in mind is that the influence this person will have on your life will be great, so make sure you seek someone who is experienced and wise.

Seek God's presence in your interactions with your new support system, inviting their guidance and helping you to align God's plan for your marriage. This will give you the ability to reciprocate the love and support you are receiving and foster a cycle of mutual encouragement with one another.

PRAYER:

Heavenly Father,

We approach you with hearts full of gratitude for the companionship and support you have provided on our journey of marriage. Thank you for the relationships that have uplifted and encouraged us along the way.

Lord, as we reflect on Ecclesiastes 4:9, we recognize the wisdom in building a strong support system for our marriage. We understand that just as two are better than one, the presence of meaningful relationships enhances our journey.

Guide us in identifying friends and mentors who share our values and contribute to our growth as a couple. May these relationships provide a nurturing environment where our love can flourish.

As we commit to nurturing these connections, we invite your guidance in our interactions. May our conversations be filled with wisdom and understanding. May our bonds be strengthened through mutual encouragement and support.

Father, we pray for the discernment to recognize relationships that align with your plan for our marriage. Help us to be intentional in cultivating connections that uplift and inspire us.

In moments of vulnerability, may our support system be a source of comfort and guidance. In moments of joy, may we celebrate together, sharing in the rewards of our toil as a united team.

We ask for your wisdom in reciprocating the love and support we receive. May our interactions be marked by a spirit of generosity and gratitude.

In Jesus' name, we pray,

Amen.

Closing Thoughts:

Building a strong support system is an integral aspect of nurturing a thriving marriage. Through the wisdom of Ecclesiastes 4:9, you understand the value of companionship and the rewards it brings to your journey together. By reflecting on meaningful relationships, seeking God's guidance through prayer, and intentionally cultivating connections that uplift and encourage, you create a nurturing environment where your love can flourish and grow. May this week be a time of deepened gratitude, enriched connections, and renewed dedication to building a strong support system that enhances the beauty and strength of your marriage.

EMBRACING CHANGE AND GROWTH

Scripture: Isaiah 43:19

*Behold, I am doing a new thing; now it springs forth, do you not perceive it?
I will make a way in the wilderness and rivers in the desert.*

Devotion:

Life is a journey of constant change and evolution, and in the midst of change, we find growth. Isaiah 43:19 reminds us of the divine promise that God is continuously doing new things, making paths in the wilderness and bringing forth rivers in the desert. In this, we see the beauty and potential of embracing change and growth, both individually and as a couple.

Change can be daunting, but it is often the catalyst for transformation and progress. Just as nature undergoes seasons of change, so do our lives. These changes provide us with opportunities to learn, adapt, and become better versions of ourselves.

As a couple, embracing change and growth requires open hearts, willingness, and a shared commitment to support each other's aspirations. When you face change together, you not only nurture your individual growth but also strengthen the bond that holds your partnership.

Reflection:

This week, engage in a reflective conversation with your partner about personal growth and the changes you both aspire to make. Share your individual goals, dreams, and aspirations for the future, discussing how these contribute to your personal development.

Explore how your growth as individuals intersects with your growth as a couple. Discuss how your aspirations align, complement, and challenge each other. Consider how your shared goals can contribute to the overall well-being and strength of your relationship.

Marriage Activity:

As a marriage activity, embark on a joint creative project that symbolizes your commitment to embracing change and growth together. This could involve creating a vision board that represents your individual and shared aspirations, using images, quotes, and words that inspire and motivate you.

As you work on the vision board, share your thoughts and feelings about the changes you want to embrace and the growth you hope to achieve. Use this activity as a platform for mutual encouragement and support.

Place the completed vision board in a prominent location where you can see it daily. Let it serve as a visual reminder of your shared journey toward positive change and growth, both as individuals and as a united couple.

PRAYER:

Heavenly Father,

As we reflect on the words of Isaiah 43:19, we are reminded of your promise to make a way in the wilderness and to bring forth rivers in the desert. You are the author of new beginnings, and we trust in your guidance as we navigate the changes and growth in our lives and marriage.

Lord, change can be both exciting and challenging. It stretches us beyond our comfort zones and tests our faith. We ask for your strength and courage as we embrace the opportunities that change brings, both as individuals and as a couple.

As we engage in conversations about our personal growth goals, may our hearts be open and receptive to each other's aspirations. Help us to align our dreams with your plan for our lives, finding unity in our shared journey.

We thank you for the support system you've placed in our lives—friends, mentors, and loved ones who encourage us to embrace change and strive for growth. May these relationships continue to inspire and uplift us on this journey.

As we create a vision board together, may it serve as a visual reminder of our commitment to positive change. May it symbolize our shared determination to evolve and flourish in your love.

Guide us, Lord, as we face the unknown and step into new territories. Let your light illuminate our path, and grant us the wisdom to discern your direction.

In your name, we pray,

Amen.

Closing Thoughts:

Embracing change and growth as individuals and as a couple is a transformative practice that enriches your journey and strengthens your bond. Through the lens of Isaiah 43:19, you recognize the beauty of new beginnings and the potential that change brings.

By discussing personal growth goals, supporting each other's aspirations, and facing change with faith and courage, you create a dynamic environment where your love can continue to flourish and evolve. May this week be a time of reflection, open-hearted conversations, and a renewed dedication to embracing change and growth with anticipation and joy.

CULTIVATING A SPIRIT OF GENEROSITY

Scripture: 2 Corinthians 9:7

Each one must give as he has decided in his heart, not reluctantly or under compulsion, for God loves a cheerful giver.

Devotion:

Generosity is a virtue that reflects the essence of selflessness and compassion. It's the willingness to give freely, not out of obligation, but from a heart that overflows with love and empathy. In 2 Corinthians 9:7, we are reminded of the beauty of cheerful giving, a giving that is joyful and abundant.

As a couple, embracing a spirit of generosity can have a profound impact on your marriage and the world around you. When you give with a cheerful heart, you open the doors to deeper connections, enhanced gratitude, and a sense of purpose that extends beyond yourselves.

Reflection:

This week, take time to reflect with your partner on the various ways you can give back to your community as a couple. Explore the causes, organizations, or initiatives that resonate with both of you. Consider your unique strengths, talents, and resources that you can contribute.

Engage in a thoughtful discussion about how you can pool your efforts to make a positive impact. Brainstorm creative ways to support those in need, whether through volunteer work, donations, or acts of kindness that uplift others.

Spiritual Practice:

While prayer is a powerful spiritual practice, this week's focus on generosity invites you to take tangible actions that align with your devotion. As a couple, commit to performing acts of kindness throughout the week. These acts can be simple yet meaningful gestures that uplift and bless others.

Ideas for acts of kindness could include:

1 - Volunteering your time at a local charity or community organization.

2 - Donating to a cause or charity that is close to your heart.

3 - Offering to help a neighbor or friend in need.

4 - Writing handwritten notes of encouragement to people who may be going through a challenging time.

5 - Engaging in random acts of kindness, such as paying for someone's meal or leaving uplifting messages in public spaces.

By actively engaging in acts of kindness, you embody the spirit of generosity and cheerful giving that 2 Corinthians 9:7 encourages. Your actions become a tangible expression of your devotion and a way to make a positive impact on the lives of others.

PRAYER:

Heavenly Father,

As we delve into the depths of generosity, we are reminded of Your boundless love that knows no limits. Just as You have given us all that we have, we seek to reflect that love through our actions and attitudes.

Thank You for the gift of each other, for the partnership that is our marriage. Help us to see the opportunities around us to give joyfully, freely, and with hearts full of love. May our generosity extend beyond material possessions to include our time, our kindness, and our empathy.

Guide us, Lord, as we engage in acts of kindness throughout this week. Open our eyes to the needs of those around us, and give us the wisdom to meet those needs in ways that bring comfort, hope, and encouragement. May our actions be a reflection of Your grace, a reminder that Your love flows through us and into the lives of others.

Teach us to give not out of obligation or compulsion, but with hearts that overflow with joy. Just as 2 Corinthians 9:7 encourages us, may our giving be cheerful, a reflection of Your love that dwells within us.

As we explore ways to give back to our community as a couple, we ask for Your guidance and inspiration. Show us the paths that align with Your will, the causes that resonate with our hearts, and the people who could use our support.

Help us to be mindful of the impact our generosity can have on the world around us. May our actions inspire others to join in acts of kindness, creating a ripple effect of love and compassion that reaches far and wide.

Lord, we are grateful for the opportunity to embrace a spirit of generosity to partner with You in making a positive difference in the lives of those around us. As we commit to this week of intentional giving, may Your presence be felt in every act of kindness, and may our hearts be filled with the joy that comes from selflessly sharing with others.

In Your name, we pray,

Amen.

Closing Thoughts:

Cultivating a spirit of generosity is a powerful practice that enriches your marriage and leaves a lasting impact on the world around you. Through the lens of 2 Corinthians 9:7, you understand that cheerful giving is a reflection of God's love and His desire for us to share our blessings joyfully.

By discussing how to give back to your community as a couple and actively engaging in acts of kindness and generosity, you create a legacy of love and compassion. May this week be a time of reflection, meaningful conversations, and a renewed dedication to embracing a spirit of generosity that brings joy to your hearts and blessings to others.

OVERCOMING RESENTMENT AND BITTERNESS

Scripture: Matthew 6:14-15

For if you forgive others their trespasses, your heavenly Father will also forgive you, but if you do not forgive others their trespasses, neither will your Father forgive your trespasses.

Devotion:

Matthew 6:14-15 highlights the intricate relationship between forgiveness and our own spiritual well-being. It reminds us that forgiving others is not just a matter of resolving conflicts—it's a step toward personal liberation and a heart aligned with God's grace.

Resentment and bitterness are like toxins that seep into the core of your marriage, poisoning the love and harmony you share. However, just as toxins can be purged from the body through intentional care, forgiveness is the antidote that cleanses your relationship of negativity.

When you choose to forgive, you release the grip of bitterness and create space for healing and growth. It's not an erasure of the past but a conscious decision to unshackle yourself from the weight of resentment. In doing so, you create an environment where love, understanding, and trust can flourish.

Reflection:

Take a moment to reflect on any areas of resentment and bitterness that may have taken root in your marriage. These emotions often stem from hurtful incidents, misunderstandings, or unmet expectations. They can build over time, becoming barriers to the intimacy and connection you both desire.

In light of Matthew 6:14-15, which emphasizes the interconnectedness of forgiveness and the condition of our own forgiveness, consider discussing these feelings with your partner. Approach the conversation with a genuine desire to understand each other's perspectives and to find a path toward healing.

Marriage Activity:

As a practical step towards overcoming resentment and bitterness, embark on a joint journaling exercise. Create a shared journal where you both write down your thoughts, feelings, and reflections about the issues that have caused resentment. Use this as a safe space to express yourself honestly and without judgment.

Take turns reading each other's entries, and then engage in a heartfelt conversation about what you've written. This exercise not only provides an outlet for your emotions but also opens a dialogue for understanding and healing.

PRAYER:

Heavenly Father,

In Your boundless grace and wisdom, we come before You with open hearts, seeking Your guidance and strength as we navigate the journey of releasing resentment and bitterness from our marriage.

We acknowledge the weight that these emotions can carry, like heavy anchors holding us back from the fullness of love and connection You desire for us. We recognize that harboring these feelings not only affects our relationship with each other but also hinders our ability to experience the depth of Your forgiveness.

As we reflect on the words of Matthew 6:14-15, we understand the profound link between extending forgiveness and receiving Your forgiveness. Help us, Lord, to grasp the importance of letting go and the freedom that comes from choosing forgiveness over resentment.

Grant us the courage to address any unresolved issues that have given rise to bitterness. May our conversations be guided by empathy and a genuine desire to understand each other's perspectives. Fill our hearts with humility, allowing us to acknowledge our own shortcomings and extend grace to one another.

As we embark on the joint journaling exercise, we ask for Your presence to infuse our words. May this act of vulnerability and shared reflection pave the way for healing and understanding. Let this journal be a testament to our commitment to walk the path of forgiveness hand in hand.

Lord, we lay before You our hurts, disappointments, and grievances. We choose to release them into Your capable hands, knowing that You are the ultimate source of healing and restoration. In the light of Your love, resentment loses its grip, and bitterness gives way to a renewed sense of hope.

Guide us in this journey, Heavenly Father. Strengthen us to overcome the temptations of bitterness and resentment. Fill us with Your grace and mercy, that we may extend them freely to one another. May our marriage be a living testament to Your transformative power, a testament of love triumphing over negativity.

We thank You, Lord, for the gift of forgiveness and the opportunity to experience the beauty of reconciliation. May this week be a stepping stone toward a stronger, more vibrant marriage—one that reflects Your love and grace to the world around us.

In Your name, we pray,

Amen.

Closing Thoughts:

As you meditate on Matthew 6:14-15 and its profound message on forgiveness, remember that letting go of resentment and bitterness is a gift you give to yourselves as a couple. By addressing unresolved issues and actively seeking forgiveness, you choose to untangle the knots that have hindered your connection.

By embracing this week's practice, you take a purposeful step towards restoring the harmony and unity that define a healthy marriage. May this week be a time of introspection, honest conversations, and a deep commitment to release the anchor of resentment, allowing your relationship to sail freely toward the waters of renewal and reconciliation.

BALANCING WORK AND FAMILY LIFE

Scripture: Colossians 3:23-24

Whatever you do, work heartily, as for the Lord and not for men, knowing that from the Lord you will receive the inheritance as your reward. You are serving the Lord Christ.

Devotion:

In the fast-paced world we inhabit, the pursuit of career excellence can sometimes cast a shadow over the treasures of our family life. Colossians 3:23-24 offers a poignant reminder that our work is not solely for earthly gain—it is a means of serving the Lord Christ. This perspective shifts our focus from mere tasks to a higher purpose, infusing our endeavors with a sense of devotion and meaning.

Yet, in the midst of our work aspirations, we must also heed the call to honor our family relationships. Our true inheritance lies not in the accolades we accumulate at work, but in the moments we share with our loved ones—the laughter, the conversations, and the love that binds us.

Finding a balance between work and family is both an art and a discipline. It requires intentional effort to create space for the ones we hold dear, setting boundaries that safeguard our cherished moments together. As we embark on this journey, we reflect on our priorities, making conscious choices that align with the values we hold as individuals and as a couple.

Reflection:

Take a moment to reflect on the current state of your work-life balance. Are you dedicating ample time and energy to your family amidst your professional commitments? Are there moments when work begins to encroach upon the precious time meant for your loved ones?

In the spirit of Colossians 3:23-24, consider ways to intentionally prioritize family time. This may involve setting boundaries around work-related activities during evenings or weekends, creating designated "unplugged" moments, and seeking opportunities to engage in shared activities that strengthen the bonds of your family.

For Her

Spiritual Practice:

Take a moment to reflect on the current state of your work-life balance. Are you dedicating ample time and energy to your family amidst your professional commitments? Are there moments when work begins to encroach upon the precious time meant for your loved ones?

In the spirit of Colossians 3:23-24, consider ways to intentionally prioritize family time. This may involve setting boundaries around work-related activities during evenings or weekends, creating designated "unplugged" moments, and seeking opportunities to engage in shared activities that strengthen the bonds of your family.

PRAYER:

Heavenly Father,

As we come before You in prayer, we acknowledge Your divine presence in every facet of our lives. You are the orchestrator of time, the giver of purpose, and the source of all wisdom. We humbly seek Your guidance and grace as we strive to find a balance between our work responsibilities and the precious moments we share with our family.

In the busyness of our days, help us to remember the profound truth of Colossians 3:23-24. May our hearts be attuned to the higher purpose of our work—to serve You, our Lord Christ, with diligence and dedication. Yet, as we immerse ourselves in our tasks, grant us the wisdom to recognize the moments that truly matter—the moments spent with those we hold dear.

We confess that, at times, the demands of our careers can overshadow the treasures of our family life. We ask for forgiveness for the times we have allowed work to encroach upon the time meant for our loved ones. Empower us, dear Lord, to set healthy boundaries, create space for shared activities, and to be fully present in the presence of our family.

In the reflection of Colossians 3:23-24, we commit to approaching our work as an offering to You. With hearts full of dedication, we seek to excel in our endeavors, knowing that in doing so, we honor You. Yet, we also commit to nurturing the bonds of our family relationships, for they are the true inheritance and reward that surpasses any earthly gain.

As we engage in the spiritual practice of prayer this week, we seek Your divine wisdom. Grant us clarity as we discern how to prioritize our time, how to allocate our energy, and how to balance our commitments. May our prayers not only guide our choices but also infuse our actions with a sense of purpose and intention.

In this journey of balancing work and family life, may we find strength in Your presence. May our decisions be guided by Your wisdom, and may our relationships be nurtured by Your love. May the moments we share with our family be filled with joy, laughter, and meaningful connections. And may our work be an expression of worship, an offering of our best efforts to You.

We offer this prayer in gratitude and anticipation, knowing that with Your guidance, we can find the harmony and equilibrium that glorify You in all aspects of our lives.

In Your holy name, we pray,

Amen.

Closing Thoughts:

May this week be a time of reflection, a time to reevaluate your priorities and recalibrate your actions. In the tapestry of your lives, may work and family coexist harmoniously, each enhancing the other. As you immerse yourself in the spirit of Colossians 3:23-24, may you approach the tasks with diligence, recognizing that in your endeavors, you serve the Lord Christ.

Through prayer and intentional choices, may you strike a balance that honors both your responsibilities and your relationships. May your family thrive in the warmth of His presence, and may your work flourish as an expression of your dedication. As you navigate the complexities of balancing work and family life, may you find solace in the truth that every moment we invest in our loved ones is an eternal legacy that will transcend time.

REDISCOVERING SHARED HOBBIES

Scripture: Ecclesiastes 9:9

Enjoy life with the wife whom you love, all the days of your vain life that he has given you under the sun, because that is your portion in life and in your toil at which you toil under the sun.

Devotion:

Ecclesiastes 9:9 invites us to embrace the gift of companionship that marriage offers. It's a reminder that life is meant to be enjoyed, celebrated, and savored by the one who holds a special place in our hearts. As we journey through the ups and downs of life, the shared hobbies and interests that we engage in as a couple become the threads that weave our story together.

Rediscovering shared hobbies is a beautiful way to nurture your connection. It's a deliberate choice to invest time and energy into activities that bring you joy and strengthen your bond. Whether you're engaging in an old hobby or embarking on a new adventure, these experiences create a tapestry of memories that define your relationship.

In the busyness of life, it's easy to let these moments slip away. Yet, when we prioritize shared hobbies, we are reminded of the uniqueness of our relationship. Each shared laugh, each moment of learning, and each instance of mutual support contribute to a tapestry of love that grows richer with time.

Reflection:

Take a moment to reflect on the hobbies and interests that brought you joy as a couple in the past. Perhaps there were activities you used to love doing together—whether it was hiking, cooking, dancing, painting, or playing a musical instrument. These shared experiences are like treasures waiting to be rediscovered.

In the spirit of Ecclesiastes 9:9, consider how you can rekindle those sparks of joy. Explore new possibilities by trying activities you've never done before. Whether it's embarking on a new adventure, learning a new skill, or simply revisiting the hobbies you enjoyed in the past, the key is to do it together, cherishing each moment.

For Her

Marriage Activity:

This week's marriage activity is centered around the joy of exploration. Take time to plan and engage in a shared hobby or activity that you both enjoy. It could be as simple as taking a leisurely walk in nature, trying out a new recipe together, attending a local art class, or even stargazing under the night sky.

As you engage in this activity, focus on being fully present with each other. Let go of distractions and immerse yourselves in the experience. Use this time to create cherished memories, to laugh, to connect, and to remind yourselves of the joy that comes from sharing life's moments.

PRAYER:

Heavenly Father,

We humbly ask for Your blessing upon the journey of rediscovering shared hobbies. As we step into new experiences and revisit old joys, may our hearts be open to the beauty that surrounds us. Help us to set aside distractions and be fully present with each other, creating a space for laughter, connection, and love.

Guide us as we plan and embark on these activities. May they be moments of joy and adventure, where we find delight in each other's company and celebrate the uniqueness of our relationship. Just as You have given us the gift of companionship, may our shared hobbies be a reflection of Your love and creativity.

In the midst of these moments, we ask for Your presence to be palpable. May Your spirit infuse our interactions, deepening our bond and drawing us closer to You and to each other. Let the experiences we share be a source of inspiration, reminding us of the depth of our connection and the blessings we have in one another.

As we engage in these activities, may they serve as a reminder of the joy that comes from being intentional about our relationship. Through laughter, learning, and shared moments, may we strengthen the tapestry of our love.

In Your name, we pray,

Amen.

Closing Thoughts:

May this week be a time of exploration and reconnection, as you rediscover the joy of shared hobbies. As you engage in activities that bring you closer, may you also draw closer to the heart of your relationship. In the spirit of Ecclesiastes 9:9, may you find delight in one another's company and celebrate the gift of togetherness.

Let this week serve as a reminder of the simple yet profound truth that life is meant to be enjoyed—especially when enjoyed together. Through shared hobbies, may you create new memories, strengthen your bond, and find a deeper appreciation for the journey you are undertaking as a couple.

HONORING EACH OTHER'S LOVE LANGUAGE

Scripture: 1 Peter 4:8

Above all, keep loving one another earnestly, since love covers a multitude of sins.

Devotion:

Love is a masterpiece woven from the threads of understanding, intention, and authenticity. 1 Peter 4:8 reminds us that, above all, love is the cornerstone of our relationships—an earnest, compassionate love that covers and transcends any shortcomings.

Understanding and honoring each other's love languages is an embodiment of this transformative love. It's a commitment to listening, learning, and expressing affection in ways that hold deep meaning for our spouse. Just as we speak and listen to words in our spoken languages, embracing love languages allows us to communicate our affections in a way that resonates with the soul.

In the tapestry of our marriage, each love language is a unique hue, blending to create a vibrant and harmonious whole. As we take the time to comprehend and celebrate these languages, we are nurturing a connection that flourishes with intentionality.

Reflection:

Take a moment to reflect on your spouse's love language. Consider the ways in which they express affection and the gestures that resonate most deeply with them. Equally important, reflect on your own love language and how you prefer to give and receive love.

In the spirit of 1 Peter 4:8, embark on a journey of understanding. Engage in open and honest conversations with your spouse about your respective love languages. Share your insights, desires, and the ways in which you feel most loved. By creating this space for vulnerability, you lay the foundation for a love that is attentive and tailor-made for each other.

FOR HIM

FOR HER

Spiritual Practice:

This week's spiritual practice is focused on the beautiful journey of discovery. Set aside intentional time to explore and learn about your spouse's love language. Engage in heart-to-heart conversations that delve into the ways they feel most cherished and valued. As you listen attentively, seek to understand their preferences, desires, and gestures that resonate with their heart.

In your prayer time, ask for God's guidance in this exploration. Pray for insight, wisdom, and a receptive spirit as you uncover the unique language through which your spouse experiences and expresses love. May this process of discovery be a sacred endeavor, deepening your connection and enriching the tapestry of your relationship.

Through prayer and purposeful conversation, may you unlock the door to each other's hearts and embark on a journey of embracing and cherishing your distinct love languages.

PRAYER:

Heavenly Father,

In the sanctuary of Your presence, we come before You with hearts open to receive Your guidance and grace. We thank You for the gift of love, a language that transcends words and connects us in profound ways. As we journey through the landscape of understanding and honoring each other's love languages, we seek Your wisdom and blessing.

Your word in 1 Peter 4:8 reminds us of the power of love to cover a multitude of sins. It is a reminder that love is not only a balm for wounds but a transformative force that brings healing, renewal, and unity. We acknowledge the importance of cherishing and nurturing the love languages that speak to the depths of our souls.

As we embark on this journey of discovery, we ask for Your guidance. Open our hearts to listen and learn from one another. Grant us the ability to set aside our own preferences and desires, and, instead, attune ourselves to the unique ways in which our spouse feels cherished and valued.

In our moments of reflection, help us to uncover the nuances of each other's love languages. May our conversations be filled with vulnerability, empathy, and a deep desire to understand. As we engage in this sacred exploration, may our connection be strengthened, and our bond deepened.

As we lift our voices in prayer, we ask for Your presence to fill our conversations and interactions. Infuse our efforts with Your divine wisdom and grace. May our journey of understanding and honoring each other's love languages lead to a love that is intentional, meaningful, and transformative.

Grant us the humility to embrace new ways of expressing affection and the courage to step outside of our comfort zones. May our love be a reflection of Your love—a love that seeks to understand, uplift, and nurture.

In the name of Love Himself, we pray.

Amen.

Closing Thoughts:

May this week be a time of discovery and intentionality—an exploration of the unique love languages that define your relationship. As you engage in conversations and gestures that honor each other's preferences, may you draw closer to the heart of your spouse and to the heart of love itself.

May your journey of understanding and honoring love languages be a testament to the boundless capacity of love to heal, strengthen, and transform. And as you commit this journey to prayer, may your love be infused with divine guidance, blossoming into a symphony that harmonizes the rhythms of your hearts.

May your love languages become a bridge, connecting your souls in a dance of affection and understanding that knows no bounds.

PRIORITIZING SELF-CARE AND REST

Scripture: Psalm 127:2

It is in vain that you rise up early and go late to rest, eating the bread of anxious toil; for he gives to his beloved sleep.

Devotion:

Psalm 127:2 echoes through the corridors of time, whispering to us the profound truth that rest is a divine gift bestowed upon those whom He loves. In the context of marriage, self-care and rest become an exquisite symphony of love—a melody that enriches the union of two souls on a shared journey.

Our lives are a delicate balance of giving and receiving, of pouring out and being replenished. Just as a parched land requires rain to flourish, our hearts and spirits require the nourishment of self-care and rest to thrive. These acts of compassion toward ourselves are not indulgent; they are acts of stewardship over the vessels through which we express love to one another.

When we prioritize self-care, we affirm our worthiness to receive love and care. When we embrace rest, we acknowledge that our well-being is intrinsically linked to the health of our marriage. As we nurture our bodies, minds, and spirits, we create a fertile ground for love to bloom and flourish.

Reflection:

Take a moment to reflect on your daily routines and commitments. How often do you pause to care for your well-being, rejuvenate your spirit, and recharge your energy? How often do you prioritize rest in a world that glorifies constant activity?

In the spirit of Psalm 127:2, engage in a candid conversation with your spouse about self-care. Share the practices that bring you joy, peace, and a sense of balance. Listen attentively as your partner does the same. Together, explore ways to integrate self-care into your lives, carving out time for activities that uplift your spirits and renew your sense of purpose.

Furthermore, consider the concept of shared rest. While individual self-care is invaluable, the practice of resting together as a couple creates a unique bond. Whether it's enjoying a leisurely walk, reading a book together, or simply relishing quiet moments of togetherness, find ways to make rest a shared and cherished experience.

For Him

For Her

Marriage Activity:

This week, set aside intentional time for shared rest. Create a space where both of you can unwind and rejuvenate together. Whether it's a cozy evening at home, a peaceful nature walk, or a spa day, prioritize rest as an essential element of your marriage.

During this time, practice the art of presence. Put aside distractions and engage fully in the experience. Let laughter, conversation, and the joy of simply being together infuse the atmosphere. As you embrace shared rest, you'll not only strengthen your connection but also create lasting memories of the precious moments you've shared.

PRAYER:

Heavenly Father,

In the quiet sanctuary of Your presence, we bow before You with hearts open to receive Your grace and wisdom. We thank You for the precious gift of love that binds us as partners on this journey of life. As we reflect on the importance of self-care and rest in our marriage, we humbly seek Your guidance and blessing.

Your word in Psalm 127:2 speaks to the depths of our souls, reminding us that the pursuit of endless toil, driven by anxiety, can lead us away from the nourishing embrace of rest. In this fast-paced world, help us remember that rest is not a sign of weakness, but a sacred practice that replenishes our spirits and strengthens the bonds of love.

As we navigate the demands of our daily lives, grant us the wisdom to prioritize self-care. Open our eyes to the activities and practices that rejuvenate our bodies, minds, and souls. In caring for ourselves, may we acknowledge the sanctity of our well-being and honor the vessels through which we express love to one another.

Guide us, O Lord, as we explore ways to rest together as a couple. May our shared moments of relaxation be a testament to the beauty of togetherness and the joy of being fully present in each other's company. Help us create a haven of peace where laughter, conversation, and cherished memories can flourish.

As we lift our voices in prayer, we seek Your peace and rejuvenation. Grant us the ability to release the burdens of anxiety and worry, replacing them with the serenity that comes from trusting in Your provision. May our pursuit of self-care and rest be guided by Your loving hand, leading us to a place of restoration and renewal.

In the depth of our love, may we find the courage to prioritize self-care without guilt, and to embrace rest as a gift from Your hands. As we embark on this journey of nourishing our well-being, may our marriage be a testament to the profound truth that a love nurtured in rest and self-care is a love that blossoms and flourishes.

In Your name, we pray.

Amen.

Closing Thoughts:

May this week be a sanctuary of self-care and shared rest—a respite where you honor the sanctity of your well-being and the bond you share. As you engage in meaningful conversations and create moments of restful togetherness, may you discover the beauty of being fully present in each other's company.

In your pursuit of self-care and rest, may you find the courage to release the burdens of anxious toil and the wisdom to embrace the gift of rejuvenation. Just as Psalm 127:2 reminds us, rest is a manifestation of love—a divine embrace that cradles our hearts and invites us to experience true nourishment.

May your self-care practices and shared moments of rest become a testimony to the depth of your love—a love that treasures, cherishes, and seeks the well-being of one another.

CREATING A VISION FOR YOUR MARRIAGE

Scripture: Proverbs 29:18

Where there is no prophetic vision the people cast off restraint, but blessed is he who keeps the law.

Devotion:

In the tapestry of every successful endeavor, a vision serves as the guiding thread that weaves purpose and direction. Just as a master artist envisions a masterpiece before the first stroke of the brush, so too should a married couple envision the masterpiece they wish to create with their lives together.

Proverbs 29:18 reminds us that a prophetic vision is a source of blessing. It is the seed from which intentionality and purpose blossom. a shared vision for your marriage is a testament to your commitment to a journey hand in hand, guided by a common purpose that ignites your passions and fuels your aspirations.

Your shared vision is a reflection of the unique strengths and qualities each of you brings to the union. As you discuss your long-term goals, dreams, and desires, you are not only shaping your future but also deepening your connection. Through honest conversation and mutual understanding, you build a bridge between your individual journeys and forge a path of unity.

Reflection:

Pause for a moment and consider the future you envision for your marriage. What are the dreams that you hold dear? What are the aspirations that stir your hearts? Take time to engage in a heartfelt conversation with your spouse about your long-term goals. Share your hopes, dreams, and desires openly and honestly.

In the spirit of Proverbs 29:18, explore the ways in which your shared vision can shape your daily lives. Discuss how your goals align with your values, how they impact your decisions, and how they contribute to the legacy you wish to leave. By weaving your aspirations into the fabric of your marriage, you build a sturdy foundation for your journey together.

Spiritual Practice:

This week, embark on a transformative journey of casting a shared vision for your marriage. Find a quiet and intentional space where you can both engage in this meaningful exercise together.

Reflect and Share: Begin by individually reflecting on your deepest desires and aspirations for your marriage. Then, come together and take turns sharing your thoughts. Listen attentively, affirming each other's dreams without judgment.

Craft Your Vision: Identify common themes and goals from your discussions. Collaboratively articulate a concise shared vision statement that captures the essence of what you both envision for your marriage.

Set Goals and Pray: From your shared vision, outline specific goals that align with your aspirations. As a concluding step, bow in prayer, seeking God's guidance and blessing on the vision you've created, and ask for strength to journey forward together.

In casting a shared vision, you nurture a foundation that fuels your partnership with purpose and unity, echoing the wisdom of Proverbs 29:18. This practice not only strengthens your bond but also illuminates the path toward a fulfilling and blessed marriage.

PRAYER:

Heavenly Father,

In this sacred moment of togetherness, we humbly approach Your throne of grace. We thank You for the gift of love that intertwines our hearts and spirits in this blessed union of marriage. As we embark on the journey of casting a shared vision for our partnership, we invite Your presence to guide and illuminate our path.

You remind us in Proverbs 29:18 of the power of a prophetic vision—a vision that shapes destinies and blesses lives. As we reflect on our individual aspirations and dreams, may Your wisdom weave them into a beautiful tapestry of shared purpose. Help us to listen with open hearts, to understand without judgment, and to affirm each other's deepest desires.

As we craft a shared vision, may Your divine hand guide our words and intentions. Strengthen the bonds of unity between us as we articulate a concise vision statement that encapsulates our hopes for this journey together. May this vision be a source of inspiration, a compass directing our steps toward a future filled with love, growth, and fulfillment.

Lord, from this shared vision, we outline specific goals that reflect the desires of our hearts. In this moment of prayer, we lay these aspirations before You, seeking Your blessing and guidance. May You infuse our goals with purpose, and may Your light shine upon the path we are carving.

Grant us the strength and resilience to pursue this shared vision, even when challenges arise. May our partnership be marked by grace, understanding, and a commitment to nurture each other's dreams. In the midst of our journey, may Your presence be our constant companion, reassuring us of Your loving guidance.

As we conclude this time of reflection and prayer, we offer our hearts to You, trusting that the vision we've cast is aligned with Your divine plan for our lives. May our shared vision serve as a testimony of Your love and wisdom at work within our marriage.

In Your holy name, we pray.

Amen.

Closing Thoughts:

May this week be a time of profound reflection and shared dreaming—a time when you carve out space to envision the beautiful tapestry of your life together. As you embrace the wisdom of Proverbs 29:18, may your shared vision become a source of inspiration and blessing, guiding you toward a future that is rich in purpose and love.

May your conversations be filled with hope and anticipation as you discuss your long-term goals and aspirations. And as you engage in the spiritual practice of prayer and reflection, may your hearts be open to divine guidance and revelation, bringing clarity and unity to the vision you are crafting.

In the tapestry of your marriage, may your shared vision be a masterpiece that reflects the beauty of your love and the profound journey you are undertaking together.

CELEBRATING YOUR MILESTONES

Scripture: Psalm 145:4

One generation shall commend your works to another, and shall declare your mighty acts.

Devotion:

In the tapestry of your marriage, there are moments woven with threads of joy, challenges, and shared experiences that have shaped your unique love story. Psalm 145:4 reminds us of the beauty in acknowledging and celebrating the significant milestones in our journey together. These milestones are not mere markers in time, but they are opportunities to honor the transformative power of love, commitment, and shared growth.

Life's journey is a blend of hills and valleys, each contributing to the intricate design of your marriage. As you stand at this juncture, take a moment to reflect on the path you've traveled. The commitment you made to each other on your wedding day has led to a series of beautiful moments that deserve to be cherished and celebrated. These milestones are like stepping stones, leading you to a deeper connection and a more profound understanding of one another.

Reflection:

In the busyness of life, it's easy to overlook the significance of your journey. Amid responsibilities and routine, pause to reflect on the remarkable moments that have brought you to where you are today. Think back to the day you exchanged vows, the birth of your children, the challenges you overcame, and the laughter you shared. Each of these moments has contributed to the mosaic of your marriage.

As you reflect, let gratitude fill your hearts. Gratitude is a powerful force that shifts your perspective, allowing you to focus on the blessings you've received. Express thankfulness for the journey, for the times when your love was a rock in the storm and a source of joy in the mundane. Let the warmth of gratitude draw you closer, reminding you of the unwavering love that has guided you through the years.

Marriage Activity:

This week, engage in an activity that honors your journey and celebrates the milestones you've achieved. Create a "Milestone Memory Box" together. Find a beautiful box or container that resonates with both of you. Gather items that symbolize significant moments—a photograph from your wedding day, a handwritten note from a memorable anniversary, a trinket from a special trip, or a drawing from your child.

As you select these items, let each one evoke conversations and memories. Share stories, laughter, and perhaps even a few tears as you recount the experiences that have molded your marriage. Take your time curating this collection, allowing it to reflect the depth and breadth of your love journey.

Once your Milestone Memory Box is complete, find a prominent place in your home to display it. Let it be a visible reminder of the remarkable journey you've undertaken together—a tangible representation of the moments that have shaped your story.

PRAYER:

Heavenly Father,

In the presence of Your boundless love, we come before You with hearts brimming with gratitude. You have walked alongside us through every milestone, every triumph, and every moment of growth. As we reflect on our journey, we are reminded of Your faithfulness and grace that have illuminated our path.

Thank You for the moments that have shaped us—a tapestry woven with threads of joy, challenges, and shared experiences. We are grateful for the strength You've granted us, the lessons we've learned, and the love that continues to flourish.

As we celebrate our milestones, may our hearts overflow with thanksgiving. Help us cherish the memories we've created and the bond that has deepened with each passing day. May our Milestone Memory Box be a cherished treasure, a visual testament to the chapters we've written together.

Lord, we lift our voices in prayer, thanking You for the blessings we've received and the growth we've experienced. May our marriage continue to be a canvas for Your mighty acts, a canvas we paint with love, trust, and a shared purpose.

In Your holy name, we pray.

Amen.

Closing Thoughts:

As you celebrate the milestones of your journey, remember that each moment, whether big or small, contributes to the rich tapestry of your love story. Just as Psalm 145:4 encourages, may you declare the mighty acts of God through your marriage, testifying to His faithfulness. Let the Milestone Memory Box serve as a reminder that your love is a beautiful mosaic, woven together by grace, shared experiences, and a commitment to journeying together. May your celebration of milestones deepen your bond and inspire you to continue creating a legacy of love for generations to come.

CULTIVATING HUMILITY AND GRACE

Scripture: 1 Peter 5:6

Humble yourselves, therefore, under the mighty hand of God so that at the proper time he may exalt you.

Devotion:

Humility and grace are threads of utmost significance. They are not mere virtues; they are powerful forces that shape the very foundation of your relationship. Just as a garden thrives when it receives the nurturing care of a skilled gardener, your marriage flourishes when you intentionally cultivate humility and extend grace to one another.

The Scripture in 1 Peter 5:6 provides profound insights into these virtues. It reminds us that humility is not a sign of weakness, but rather a reflection of strength and wisdom. Humility requires the courage to acknowledge that none of us stands above the other and that each partner has unique strengths and perspectives that contribute to the intricate design of your partnership.

Grace, as well, is a cornerstone of love. It's the art of bestowing kindness, understanding, and forgiveness, even when it's undeserved. Just as God's grace covers our shortcomings, so too should our grace envelop our spouse's imperfections. When grace flows freely within a marriage, it becomes a haven of safety and acceptance—a space where both partners can grow and evolve without fear of judgment.

Reflection:

Embracing humility and grace requires introspection and honest dialogue. Take time to reflect on your interactions and identify areas where these virtues may need further nurturing. Perhaps there have been moments when pride or stubbornness prevented open communication, or times when grace was overshadowed by frustration.

In this reflection, approach the conversation with a heart eager to learn and grow. Create an atmosphere of safety where both partners can openly share their thoughts and feelings. Be attentive to each other's words, seeking not just to be heard, but to truly understand.

As you discuss these areas, remember that humility does not diminish your worth; rather, it enriches the depth of your connection. Likewise, grace is not a sign of surrender; it's a powerful expression of love that allows your marriage to thrive even in the face of challenges.

Spiritual Practice:

In the act of humility, we will learn the Palms Down, Palms Up Prayer. This prayer helps us to remain humble and encouraging while at the same time having the ability to release whatever is harmful to the marriage.

Begin by sitting in a comfortable chair, facing one another, and placing your palms down on your own legs to symbolize the desire to release your concerns to God. Begin by asking the Holy Spirit to show you what the two of you will need to let go of. Is there anything in your relationship that is blocking your relationship with Christ?

Then, turn your palms face up in an act of humility, releasing any worries, confessing any sins, and revealing a desire to receive from God. It's a simple way to come humbly before God while emptying your hearts at the same time. Together, you can give God whatever is bothering you and whatever is stressing you out, while learning to receive God's forgiveness, peace, love, truth, and rest.

PRAYER:

Heavenly Father,

We come before You with hearts humbled by Your boundless love and grace. As we reflect on the virtues of humility and grace, we recognize their profound significance in our marriage. You have shown us the way, teaching us that true strength lies in the gentleness of humility and the generosity of grace.

Lord, we acknowledge that we are imperfect beings, prone to pride and self-centeredness. In our journey as a couple, we have encountered moments when humility was needed—to step back, to listen, and to put the needs of our spouse before our own. Grant us the wisdom to recognize these moments and the courage to embrace humility, knowing that it is a reflection of Your character.

We also lift up the virtue of grace—a gift that mirrors Your unfailing love for us. Just as You have lavished Your grace upon us, help us to extend grace to one another. May our words and actions be infused with kindness, understanding, and forgiveness. In times of disagreement, may grace be the bridge that fosters understanding and reconciliation.

Lord, in our pursuit of humility and grace, we seek Your guidance. Strengthen us to overcome the obstacles that hinder these virtues from flourishing in our marriage. Grant us the ability to communicate openly and honestly, to set aside pride, and to embrace vulnerability. Empower us to be quick to forgive, to let go of grudges, and to choose love above all else.

As we bow our hearts before You, we envision our marriage as a tapestry woven with threads of humility and grace. May it be a testament to Your transformative power, a beacon of light and love in a world often clouded by pride and division.

In moments of strength and moments of weakness, may humility be our anchor, and may grace be our compass. Help us to cultivate these virtues daily, shaping our marriage into a haven of understanding, acceptance, and unwavering love.

We thank You, Lord, for the gift of one another, for the journey we've embarked upon, and for the opportunity to reflect Your character through humility and grace. May our marriage be a source of inspiration to others, showcasing the beauty that emerges when we choose to walk humbly and extend grace, just as You have done for us.

In Your precious name, we pray.

Amen.

Closing Thoughts:

The journey of cultivating humility and grace is not a destination; it's a continuous exploration. It's a path marked by growth, challenges, and moments of profound connection. Just as a skilled gardener tends to their garden with diligence, may you tend to your marriage with the same care and intentionality.

As you nurture humility and extend grace, you create a legacy of love that transcends individual actions and disagreements. Your marriage becomes a radiant testament to the transformative power of Christ-like virtues. Let humility and grace be the guiding stars that illuminate your journey, drawing you closer to each other and to the heart of the One who is the ultimate source of humility and grace.

TRANSFORMING TRIALS INTO TRIUMPHS

Scripture: Romans 8:28

And we know that for those who love God all things work together for good, for those who are called according to his purpose.

Devotion:

Life is a journey filled with highs and lows, peaks and valleys. Marriage, a beautiful union between two souls, is no exception. We often envision our journey together as a path adorned with roses, where love and laughter fill the air. But the reality is, that our path can sometimes be paved with challenges and hardships that put our commitment and love to the test.

Yet, in the midst of these trials, we are not left to navigate alone. Romans 8:28 reminds us that God is always at work, orchestrating His purpose in every aspect of our lives, including our marriage. "And we know that in all things God works for the good of those who love him, who have been called according to his purpose."

Trials are not meant to break us; they are meant to shape us. They provide opportunities for growth, strength, and character development. When we face challenges in our marriage, it's easy to become overwhelmed by the weight of the moment and lose sight of the bigger picture. However, God's promise in Romans 8:28 assures us that even in the midst of difficulties, He is working for our good.

Reflection:

Consider the challenges you've faced together as a couple. Remember the times when communication broke down, when you felt distant from each other, or when external circumstances brought stress into your lives. As you reflect on these moments, also reflect on the ways you overcame them. Did you communicate openly and honestly? Did you learn to lean on each other for support? Did you seek God's guidance through prayer?

Trials have a way of revealing our true selves and the depth of our commitment. They show us where we need to grow, where we need to extend grace, and where we need to lean on God for strength. Through these challenges, God invites us to discover hidden strengths within ourselves and our marriage.

Marriage Activity:

In line with the theme of Romans 8:28, this week's marriage activity involves creating a unique "Triumphs and Trials" time capsule. Find a special box or container that you can dedicate to this purpose. Gather together some meaningful items that represent both the triumphs and trials you've experienced throughout the year.

For the "Triumphs" section: Include items that symbolize moments of joy, achievement, and growth in your marriage. This could be a photo from a memorable vacation, a thank-you note, or a token of a significant accomplishment.

For the "Trials" section: Include items that represent challenges you've faced and over-come together. This might be a handwritten note about a difficult time you navigated as a couple, a reminder of a lesson learned through adversity, or a quote that inspired you during tough moments.

Place these items in the time capsule, and write heartfelt letters to each other. In your letters, express your gratitude for the triumphs and the lessons learned from the trials. Seal the time capsule and set a date in the future when you'll open it together to revisit the contents and reflect on how God's hand was at work in both the highs and lows of your journey.

This activity not only offers a unique way to reflect on the theme of Romans 8:28 but also creates a tangible reminder of God's faithfulness in transforming all experiences into something meaningful and purposeful.

PRAYER:

Heavenly Father,

As we approach this week with hearts full of gratitude and reflection, we thank You for the journey that this year has been for our marriage. Your promise in Romans 8:28 reassures us that all things work together for good for those who love You and are called according to Your purpose. We stand in awe of Your faithfulness in every triumph and trial we've encountered.

Lord, as we embark on the unique "Triumphs and Trials" time capsule activity, we invite Your presence into this process. As we gather items that represent the highs and lows of our journey, we're reminded that You have been with us every step of the way. We place these tokens of our experiences into this capsule, entrusting them to Your care.

In the triumphs, we've seen Your blessings abound. We're grateful for the moments of joy, growth, and accomplishment that have illuminated our path. We thank You for every answered prayer, every smile shared, and every victory that has strengthened the bond of our marriage.

In the trials, we've witnessed Your grace sustaining us. We remember the challenges we faced, the lessons we've learned, and the strength we've found in leaning on You. Just as You have carried us through the storms, we trust that You will continue to guide us into the future.

Lord, as we write letters to each other, expressing our gratitude for the triumphs and the wisdom gained from the trials, we pray that these words will be a testament to Your goodness. May this time capsule serve as a reminder that You are the Master Weaver, intricately crafting the tapestry of our lives.

We dedicate this activity to You, Lord. As we seal this time capsule, we also seal our commitment to continue seeking Your will for our marriage. May the day we open it again be filled with gratitude and joy, knowing that Your hand was guiding us all along.

In Jesus' name, we pray.

Amen.

Closing Thoughts:

As we journey through the ups and downs of marriage, let Romans 8:28 be our anchor. Let it remind us that even in the midst of trials, God is at work. Just as a skilled artist transforms rough stones into precious gems, God can transform our challenges into opportunities for growth, love, and triumph. Trust that His purpose is unfolding in your marriage, and embrace each trial as a stepping stone toward a stronger, more resilient relationship.

SHARING YOUR
SPIRITUAL JOURNEY

Scripture: 1 John 1:7

But if we walk in the light, as he is in the light, we have fellowship with one another, and the blood of Jesus his Son cleanses us from all sin.

Devotion:

In marriage, the threads of faith are intricately woven, creating a bond that transcends the physical and touches the spiritual. Just as a tree draws nourishment from its roots, your marriage draws strength and vitality from the deep wellspring of your shared spiritual journey. 1 John 1:7 sheds light on the beauty of this journey, reminding us that as we walk in the light of Christ, we experience fellowship with one another.

Your spiritual journey is a dynamic, evolving narrative—a story of growth, reflection, and discovery. Your individual walks with God have likely seen peaks of joy and valleys of challenge, and as a couple, these journeys merge to form a tapestry of shared experiences, beliefs, and values.

Reflection:

Set aside a moment to reflect on the path your spiritual journeys have taken. How has your faith evolved over the years? In what ways has your relationship with God influenced the way you approach challenges and celebrations in your marriage? Reflect on the moments when your faith provided solace and guidance, helping you navigate the twists and turns of life together.

As you discuss your spiritual journeys, approach the conversation with openness and curiosity. Share stories of significant milestones, times of doubt, and moments of profound connection with your faith. Listen attentively to your spouse's journey, respecting their experiences and perspectives.

Remember, this reflection is not about comparison, but about understanding. Each of you brings a unique lens through which you perceive the divine, and this diversity enriches your collective journey. Embrace these differences, knowing that they contribute to the vibrant tapestry of your marriage.

Spiritual Practice:

Embark on the spiritual practice of Examen together. Start by finding a quiet place and begin to ask the Holy Spirit to guide the two of you on a time of reflection. Close your eyes and take a moment to review what has happened in the last 24 hours.

When you are ready, maybe set a timer, and open your eyes. Begin to ask each other some questions. Examples of these questions can be: What inspired gratitude today? Did something painful happen? Is there a moment you regret? Did you sense God's nearness?

You may think of other questions that can be asked. When you are done, spend some time thanking God for His presence throughout the day and praying for one another based on the answers to your questions.

PRAYER:

Heavenly Father,

In the radiant presence of Your light, we come before You as a couple united in faith. We are grateful for the intertwining journeys of our hearts, and the shared steps we've taken on this spiritual path. As we reflect on the beauty of our individual walks with You and the way they have shaped our marriage, we are humbled by Your grace.

Thank You for the moments of revelation and transformation we've experienced in Your presence. We acknowledge that our faith journeys have been marked by peaks of joy and valleys of uncertainty. Yet, through it all, Your guiding light has illuminated our way, and we have found fellowship not only with You but also with each other.

As we discuss our spiritual evolution, grant us hearts open to understanding and empathy. May our reflections on our faith journey strengthen our bond and deepen our appreciation for the unique perspectives we bring to our marriage. Help us to listen with love and to share with vulnerability, nurturing a space of trust where our stories can intertwine.

In the sanctuary of prayer, we lift up our desire for a deeper spiritual connection as a couple. We thank You for the blessings of unity and shared faith that have enriched our relationship. As we pray, we ask for Your continued guidance. May Your Spirit infuse our marriage with a sense of purpose, aligning our steps as we seek Your truth together.

Grant us wisdom to support and encourage one another in our individual walks of faith. May our love and respect for each other's journey deepen, and may our commitment to seeking Your light together be unwavering. Just as You cleanse us from sin, may our shared faith cleanse our hearts of any barriers that hinder our connection.

As we navigate the tapestry of our marriage, may Your light illuminate every thread, making our bond stronger and our love more profound. May our spiritual journey be a testimony to the transformative power of Your presence in our lives.

In the name of Your Son, Jesus Christ, we pray.

Amen.

Closing Thoughts:

Your shared spiritual journey is a treasure—an ongoing narrative that weaves faith into the very fabric of your marriage. As you reflect on the path you've walked and the path that lies ahead, remember that the beauty of this journey is not just in the destination, but in the steps you take together.

May your faith journey be a source of inspiration, strength, and encouragement. And as you continue to walk hand in hand, may your connection deepen, and your love for one another be illuminated by the eternal light of Christ's love.

As you reflect, share, and pray, may your marriage be a testament to the truth that walking in the light of Christ brings not only fellowship with each other but also a cleansing and renewal that strengthens your bond.

113

BUILDING A LEGACY OF LOVE

Scripture: Psalm 103:17

The steadfast love of the Lord is from everlasting to everlasting on those who fear him, and his righteousness to children's children.

Devotion:

Your marriage is a brushstroke—a vibrant hue that adds depth and beauty to the canvas of generations. Psalm 103:17 speaks of the enduring love of the Lord, reaching from one generation to the next. As a couple, you have the unique opportunity to weave a legacy of love and faith that transcends the boundaries of time, leaving an indelible mark on your descendants.

A legacy is more than an inheritance of material wealth; it's a heritage of values, character, and beliefs that are passed down through the ages. Just as a torch is passed from hand to hand, your marriage can be a beacon of love and faith that lights the way for your children's children.

Reflection:

Gather as a couple to reflect on the legacy you wish to create. Engage in a thoughtful discussion about the values that are dear to your hearts and that you desire to pass on to your future generations. Consider the virtues you want to instill in your children and the principles that will guide your family through life's twists and turns.

As you share your thoughts, listen attentively to each other's aspirations. Take time to understand the significance of these values in your partner's life. Embrace the opportunity to explore the common ground you share and honor the differences that enrich your marriage.

For Him

For Her

Marriage Activity:

Engage in a meaningful activity that connects your past, present, and future—a family tree creation. Together, explore your family lineage, discussing the stories and values that have been passed down through the generations. As you trace the branches of your family tree, reflect on the significance of your heritage and the impact it has on your lives.

As you delve into your family history, take the opportunity to dream about the future. Imagine the branches that will extend from your own union, branching out to encompass future generations. Envision the legacy of love, faith, and values that you desire to cultivate and pass on.

Gather art supplies and create a visual representation of your family tree. Include the names of your ancestors, along with significant dates and milestones. As you craft this visual legacy, discuss the lessons and stories that have resonated with you and the ones you wish to instill in the hearts of your descendants.

Incorporate your dreams for the future into the family tree. Share your aspirations for your children, grandchildren, and beyond. Discuss the values and principles that you hope will guide and shape the generations to come.

Hang your completed family tree in a prominent place in your home—a daily reminder of the legacy you are building. Let it inspire conversations and moments of reflection as you continue to nurture and strengthen your marriage, leaving an enduring mark on the tapestry of time.

<h1 style="text-align:center">PRAYER:</h1>

Heavenly Father,

With hearts full of gratitude and reverence, we approach You as stewards of a legacy that spans generations. Thank You for the steadfast love that flows through our lineage, connecting us to those who came before us and those who will follow.

As we explore our family history and envision the future, we are reminded of the profound impact our lives have on the tapestry of time. We pray that our family tree may be a testament to Your grace and a reflection of the values that are dear to Your heart.

Guide our hands as we create a visual representation of our family tree. May this artistic expression be a symbol of the intricate bonds that tie us to our ancestors and the generations that will emerge from our union. As we craft this legacy, infuse it with Your love and wisdom.

In our dreams for the future, we humbly submit our aspirations into Your hands. May the values we hold dear—love, faith, compassion, and resilience—take root and flourish in the hearts of our descendants. May our legacy be a beacon of light, guiding them through life's journey.

As we hang this family tree in our home, may it serve as a reminder of the heritage we carry and the legacy we are building. May it inspire us to continue nurturing our marriage, with a deep commitment to leaving a lasting mark on the lives that follow.

In Your name, we pray.

Amen.

Closing Thoughts:

As you embark on the journey of building a legacy of love and faith, remember that your actions today shape the stories that will be told for generations to come. Your marriage is a vessel through which the currents of love and faith flow, touching lives that you may never meet.

May your legacy be a testament to the steadfast love of the Lord, a legacy that weaves threads of faith, hope, and compassion into the fabric of your family's story. Just as Psalm 103:17 promises, may your marriage's impact be felt from everlasting to everlasting, leaving a trail of love that spans the ages.

LETTING GO OF CONTROL

Scripture: Proverbs 3:5

Trust in the Lord with all your heart, and do not lean on your own understanding.

Devotion:

We often find ourselves entangled in the threads of control—striving to direct outcomes, manipulate circumstances, and foresee every twist and turn. Yet, the wisdom of Proverbs 3:5 calls us to a higher way—a way of trust, surrender, and relinquishing control to the One who holds the threads of our existence.

Marriage, a union of two souls on a shared journey, provides ample opportunities for us to confront our tendencies toward control. Our desire to ensure our partner's happiness, secure our future, or navigate challenges according to our understanding can lead us down a path of frustration and anxiety.

Reflection:

Sit down with your partner for an open and honest reflection on the ways control may be manifesting in your marriage. Are there areas where you're trying to orchestrate outcomes, perhaps out of fear or a desire for security? Is there a sense of unease when circumstances unfold beyond your grasp?

As you share your thoughts, practice active listening, seeking to understand each other's perspectives. Honesty and vulnerability are key to unraveling the grip of control. Explore how these tendencies may impact your relationship and unearth the seeds of discontent they may sow.

In the midst of this discussion, embrace the liberating truth that surrendering control doesn't equate to helplessness. Instead, it's an invitation to trust—a trust that transcends human understanding and taps into the divine wisdom that orchestrates the symphony of life.

Consider the journey your marriage has taken thus far. Reflect on the times when circumstances unfolded in ways you hadn't anticipated, yet ultimately led to growth, resilience, and unforeseen blessings. Embrace these moments as evidence that letting go of control allows space for God's providence to weave His masterpiece.

Spiritual Practice:

We live in a noisy world, and because of this, we become uncomfortable in the midst of silence. However, in order to hear God speaking to our hearts, we need to learn the spiritual practice of silence. To be able to hear God's voice above the noise.

This week, write down the noise that is in your head. You will notice that when you try to quiet yourself, voices of doubt, worry, or even anxiety may creep in. That is okay. As you and your partner sit in quiet, have a pen and paper ready. Whatever thoughts enter your mind, quickly write them down, and then clear your mind again.

After ten minutes, share your list of distracting thoughts and discuss what they tell you about your life. What do they tell you about your relationship with God? Then, help one another to improve.

PRAYER:

Heavenly Father,

In our lives and our marriage, we humbly come before You, acknowledging the threads of control that we often weave into the fabric of our existence. Your word in Proverbs 3:5 reminds us to trust in You with all our hearts, and we confess that, at times, we have leaned on our own understanding, attempting to manipulate outcomes according to our limited perspectives.

Today, we surrender the threads of control into Your capable hands. We lay down our anxieties, fears, and desires for certainty, recognizing that Your wisdom surpasses our own and Your ways are higher than ours. Teach us to release our grip on the illusion of control and embrace the freedom that comes from trusting in Your divine providence.

As we reflect on our marriage, we recognize the moments when our attempts to control have led to tension, frustration, and a sense of disconnection. We ask for Your forgiveness for the times we have allowed our desire for control to overshadow the beauty of partnership and mutual submission.

Grant us the grace to be vulnerable with one another as we discuss the ways control may manifest in our relationship. May our communication be filled with understanding, compassion, and a commitment to let go of the patterns that hinder our growth as a couple.

As we embark on this journey of surrender, we pray for Your guidance. Empower us to relinquish control in areas where we need to place our trust in You. Strengthen our faith as we navigate the uncertainties of life, confident that You are weaving a masterpiece of love, grace, and purpose in our marriage.

In our moments of prayer, we symbolically release our grasp on control. Just as we open our hands, we also open our hearts to Your divine direction. May our surrender be an act of worship, a testament to our faith in Your unwavering love and sovereign plan.

As we continue on this sacred journey of marriage, may our hearts be attuned to Your voice, our steps guided by Your wisdom, and our souls anchored in the truth that You are the ultimate Weaver of our story. In relinquishing control, we find true freedom, and in trusting You, we discover the abundant life You have prepared for us.

In the name of Your Son, Jesus Christ, we pray.

Amen.

Closing Thoughts:

As you navigate the delicate dance of marriage, remember that letting go of control is an act of faith—an acknowledgment that your partnership is held in the loving embrace of a higher power. Just as Proverbs 3:5 encourages us to trust with all our hearts, may your marriage be a testament to the beauty that unfolds when two hearts relinquish control and place their trust in the hands of the Divine Weaver.

THE POWER OF LAUGHTER AND JOY

Scripture: Proverbs 17:22

A joyful heart is good medicine, but a crushed spirit dries up the bones.

Devotion:

In the symphony of life, laughter, and joy compose a harmonious melody that uplifts, connects, and heals. Just as Proverbs 17:22 proclaims, a joyful heart is a remedy that brings vitality and strength, not only to our physical well-being but also to the very fabric of our relationships. In the beautiful tapestry of marriage, the threads of laughter and joy weave moments of connection, lightness, and resilience.

Reflection:

Pause for a moment and reflect on the laughter that has graced your marriage—the shared jokes, the lighthearted banter, the moments of uncontrollable giggles. These instances are not mere coincidences; they are threads of joy carefully woven by the Master Weaver, binding your hearts in a tapestry of delight.

Yet, life's demands and challenges can sometimes overshadow the joy that naturally resides within us. The toils of daily routines, the weight of responsibilities, and the world's uncertainties can cast a shadow on the landscape of our hearts. In these moments, it becomes crucial to intentionally cultivate laughter and joy.

Make a conscious effort to infuse your days with moments of shared laughter. Explore activities that tickle your funny bone and bring out your inner child—watch a comedy show, engage in playful games, or reminisce about humorous memories. Create an environment where laughter is not only welcomed but celebrated as a means of deepening your connection.

Joy is not solely dependent on circumstances; it is also a perspective—a lens through which we choose to view the world. Seek out the small, everyday joys that grace your lives—a sunrise, a warm cup of coffee, a heartfelt conversation. Embrace gratitude as a pathway to joy, shifting your focus from what's lacking to the abundance that surrounds you.

FOR HER

Marriage Activity:

Engage in an activity that encapsulates the essence of joy in your marriage—a Joyful Jar. Find a decorative jar and colorful pieces of paper. Set aside time with your partner to individually jot down moments, quotes, or experiences that bring joy to your hearts. These can be anything from shared adventures to endearing pet antics.

As you compile these joyful snippets, you're not only documenting the laughter and joy that define your relationship but also creating a reservoir of positivity to draw from during challenging times. Place the jar in a visible spot in your home as a tangible reminder of the joy that is inherent in your union.

PRAYER:

Heavenly Father,

With hearts filled with gratitude, we approach Your presence, acknowledging the gift of laughter and joy that You bestow upon us. Your word reminds us that a joyful heart is a good medicine, a balm that heals and rejuvenates. We recognize that in the context of our marriage, laughter, and joy are threads that weave connection and resilience.

As we reflect on the moments of shared laughter in our journey, we are reminded of the power they hold—the power to bridge gaps, dissolve tensions, and create lasting memories. We pray for the wisdom to intentionally cultivate these moments, to prioritize the playfulness that ignites our spirits and deepens our bond.

Grant us the grace to find joy not only in grand gestures but also in the simple, everyday moments that often go unnoticed. Help us to view life through the lens of gratitude, recognizing the abundance that surrounds us and the countless reasons we have to rejoice.

As we embark on the activity of creating a Joyful Jar, may this tangible representation of our joy become a wellspring of inspiration. May it serve as a constant reminder that joy is a choice—a choice that we make each day, regardless of circumstances.

In the moments of laughter, may we glimpse the beauty of Your creation and the joy that radiates from Your heart. In the moments of shared delight, may we experience a taste of the eternal joy that awaits us in Your presence.

May our marriage be a testament to the power of laughter and joy—a living expression of Your goodness and grace. May our laughter be infectious, our joy undeniable, and our hearts forever intertwined in the dance of delight.

In Your name, we pray.

Amen.

Closing Thoughts:

As you traverse the path of marriage, may the threads of laughter and joy be woven deeply into the fabric of your shared life. Remember that joy is not a fleeting emotion; it's a state of being that can infuse even the simplest moments with a sense of wonder and contentment. Embracing laughter as a means of connection and joy as a perspective can transform the way you navigate challenges and celebrate triumphs.

Just as a single thread can hold the strength to bind, each instance of shared laughter and heartfelt joy strengthens the bond between you. Your Joyful Jar stands as a testament to the resilience of your union—a collection of memories and moments that affirm the beauty of your journey.

As you continue to explore the landscape of your marriage, may you find joy in the journey itself. Cherish the moments that make you smile, treasure the conversations that make you laugh, and hold close to the truth that a joyful heart is a gift, both to yourselves and to those fortunate enough to witness your love. Let the echo of your laughter resonate through the chambers of your marriage, reminding you always of the enduring power of joy to enrich, enliven, and elevate your union.

NURTURING FRIENDSHIP IN MARRIAGE

Scripture: Proverbs 18:24

A man of many companions may come to ruin, but there is a friend who sticks closer than a brother.

Devotion:

In the bustling tapestry of life, where responsibilities, roles, and routines intertwine, friendship emerges as a cornerstone—a foundation upon which the grand edifice of marriage is built. Proverbs 18:24 illuminates the essence of a true friend—one who stands steadfast, who knows the inner workings of your heart, and who offers unwavering companionship through life's journey.

Reflection:

Take a moment to ponder the attributes of a close friend—someone who listens without judgment, who shares in your joys and sorrows, and who celebrates your victories as if they were their own. This portrait of friendship, when painted onto the canvas of marriage, creates a masterpiece of intimacy, understanding, and connection.

Friendship in marriage is not merely a label; it's a dynamic bond that requires intentional nurturing. It's about engaging in conversations that delve beyond daily tasks, exploring each other's dreams, fears, and aspirations. It's about laughing together, sharing inside jokes, and finding joy in the presence of one another.

Invest time and effort in the art of companionship. Discover shared interests and passions that ignite your spirits. Engage in activities that fuel your connection—whether it's cooking together, embarking on adventures, or simply savoring quiet moments of togetherness.

True friendship thrives on listening with empathy—a practice that involves not just hearing words, but understanding emotions and perspectives. Create a safe space for open dialogue, where vulnerability is welcomed, and hearts are heard.

Spiritual Practice:

The act of slowing down is a great way to nurture friendship in marriage. Jesus Himself occupied much of his time with preaching, teaching, and healing, and yet when he was on his way to heal a twelve-year-old girl, he stopped to speak to a woman who had touched his cloak. (Mark 5:21-33)

God doesn't want us to be in a hurry, and when we are, we often miss what is important to our spouse. Therefore, examine your activities. Is your life one big hurry mess? Take a moment and list all of your activities. How many include your spouse? How many include both your spouse and God? Together as a couple, prayerfully ask the Lord what activities he has planned for you and which ones are not important.

PRAYER:

Heavenly Father,

With hearts full of gratitude, we come before You, acknowledging the gift of friendship that graces our marriage. Your word reminds us of the rare and precious nature of a friend who sticks closer than a brother. We recognize that in the context of our marriage, this friendship is a treasure we hold dear.

As we reflect on the qualities of friendship, we see the threads of understanding, support, and unwavering companionship that have woven our hearts together. We pray for the wisdom to cultivate and nurture this friendship, to invest time, effort, and love into the bond we share.

Grant us the grace to be attentive listeners, to offer our undivided presence when our spouse speaks. May we seek not just to hear words, but to understand the emotions, hopes, and fears behind them. May our conversations be a source of connection and comfort, a reflection of the deep friendship that defines our marriage.

As we embark on the journey of fostering friendship, may we be intentional in our actions. May we engage in activities that kindle our shared interests and passions. May we find joy in the moments we spend together, whether in laughter, adventure, or quiet contemplation.

In the fabric of our friendship, may You be the Weaver who brings threads of grace, forgiveness, and patience. Teach us to extend these qualities to one another, creating a tapestry of love that withstands the tests of time.

We pray for Your blessing upon the friendship in our marriage. May it be a source of strength, a wellspring of joy, and a testament to the beauty of companionship that reflects Your divine design for love and partnership.

In Your name, we pray.

Amen.

Closing Thoughts:

As you reflect on the gift of friendship within your marriage, remember that this bond is a living entity—a garden that flourishes with care and attention. Just as a cherished friend stands by your side through thick and thin, let your marriage be a testament to the profound depth of companionship and intimacy that friendship brings. Nurture this friendship, tend to its growth, and watch it blossom into a radiant expression of love that stands as a beacon to all who witness your journey.

CULTIVATING COMPASSION AND EMPATHY

Scripture: Colossians 3:12

Put on then, as God's chosen ones, holy and beloved, compassionate hearts, kindness, humility, meekness, and patience.

Devotion:

In the garden of marriage, compassion and empathy are the tender shoots that blossom into exquisite blooms, filling the air with the sweet fragrance of understanding and support. Colossians 3:12 beckons us to don these virtues as garments of our identity—holy and beloved, chosen by God to embody compassion, kindness, humility, meekness, and patience.

Reflection:

Take a moment to reflect on instances when compassion and empathy have been beacons of light in your marriage—moments when a kind word or a gentle touch has bridged the gaps of misunderstanding and offered solace to a weary heart. These gestures, born of compassion, reflect the divine love that flows through your union.

In times of challenge or strife, empathy acts as a soothing balm, reminding us to step into our spouse's shoes and see the world through their eyes. It's a call to listen with intent, to understand without judgment, and to extend grace even when the terrain is rocky.

Cultivating compassion begins with a heart that is open and receptive. Approach your spouse with a willingness to truly hear their thoughts, feelings, and experiences. Seek to understand their perspective before seeking to be understood.

Empathy invites you to walk alongside your spouse's emotions. In moments of joy, share in their elation. In moments of sorrow, offer a shoulder to lean on. Let your presence communicate that their feelings matter and that you are a safe haven for their heart.

Marriage Activity:

Embark on a meaningful journey of extending compassion and empathy beyond the walls of your home. As a couple, identify a local charity, community organization, or volunteer opportunity that resonates with both of you. Dedicate time together to actively engage in a service project or volunteer activity.

Whether it's participating in a food drive, volunteering at a local shelter, or offering your time at a community event, this shared experience of giving back allows you to unite in compassion and empathy toward those in need. As you work together to make a positive impact, you'll not only strengthen your bond as a couple but also create a lasting legacy of love and service.

Reflect on the emotions and insights you gain from this experience. Discuss how the act of extending compassion to others outside your home has deepened your understanding of empathy, and how it has enriched your marriage with a shared sense of purpose and unity. This activity serves as a beautiful reminder that the power of compassion knows no bounds—it has the ability to uplift not only your marriage but also the lives of those you touch through your selfless actions.

PRAYER:

Heavenly Father,

With hearts full of gratitude, we approach Your presence, recognizing the divine call to embrace compassion and empathy within our marriage. Your word guides us to put on these virtues as garments of our identity, reflecting the depth of Your love for us.

As we reflect on the power of compassion, we are reminded of the countless ways it has transformed our marriage—softening disagreements, healing wounds, and creating a space of understanding. We pray for the grace to cultivate compassion intentionally, and to approach each other with hearts that are open, empathetic, and kind.

In times of challenge or misunderstanding, may we lean into empathy, seeking to understand before seeking to be understood. Grant us the wisdom to walk alongside each other's emotions, offering solace and support in moments of joy and sorrow alike.

As we embark on the activity of extending compassion beyond our home, may this shared endeavor deepen our connection and broaden our perspective. May the words we pen within its pages be a testament to the empathy that flows between us—a reminder that we are called to be vessels of Your compassion in our marriage.

We pray for Your blessing upon our journey of cultivating compassion and empathy. May these virtues continue to strengthen the bond we share, bringing us closer to You and to each other.

In Your name, we pray.

Amen.

Closing Thoughts:

As you reflect on the beauty of compassion and empathy within your marriage, may you find inspiration in the call to don these virtues as chosen and beloved children of God. Just as a garden thrives under the care of attentive hands, so does your marriage flourish when nourished by the waters of compassion and empathy. Let these virtues be your guiding stars, leading you through the terrain of challenges and joys, and may they continue to weave a tapestry of love that reflects the heart of the Divine Creator.

EMBRACING THE SEASONS OF MARRIAGE

Scripture: Psalm 34:8

Oh, taste and see that the Lord is good! Blessed is the man who takes refuge in him!

Devotion:

Marriage, like the changing seasons, is a journey of transformation—a path that winds through various landscapes of growth, challenges, joys, and sorrows. Just as each season brings its own beauty and lessons, each phase of your marriage offers unique opportunities for love to deepen and resilience to flourish.

Every season of marriage carries its own distinct qualities. Spring, like the tender buds of a new relationship, is a time of fresh beginnings, where the seeds of your love sprout and take root. Summer follows, characterized by the warmth of companionship and the blossoming of shared dreams. Autumn approaches with its own wisdom, prompting introspection and preparation for the future. Winter, while challenging, provides the chance to draw a close for warmth, support, and renewal.

Reflection:

Take a moment to reflect on the current season of your marriage. Are you in a season of spring, where new beginnings and growth abound? Or perhaps you find yourselves in the summer of your marriage, where the warmth of companionship and shared experiences fills the air. Maybe you're navigating the autumn of your marriage, where change is in the air, prompting introspection and preparation for the next phase. And, of course, there's the winter season, characterized by challenges and moments of hibernation.

Each season comes with its own set of challenges and blessings. In the spring, there's the excitement of newness, but also the uncertainty that comes with change. Summer brings the comfort of familiarity, yet it's essential to guard against complacency. Autumn invites reflection and preparation but may also trigger a sense of loss. Winter challenges your resilience, but it's a time of drawing closer for warmth and support.

Spiritual Practice:

Just as nature's seasons are under the divine order, so are the seasons of your marriage. Take refuge in Psalm 34:8, "Oh, taste and see that the Lord is good!" Whatever season you find yourselves in, approach it with open hearts and a desire to taste and see the goodness that God has placed before you. Seek His guidance in navigating the challenges and embracing the blessings of each season.

The spiritual practice of gratitude is a reminder of the blessings in each of our seasons. This week, every time you walk in the door of your home, look around and begin to count your blessings. You might be going through a tough season in your marriage. This will remind you of the many blessings that God has given you.

PRAYER:

Heavenly Father,

In the ever-changing journey of our marriage, we come before You with hearts full of gratitude. Just as the seasons of nature reflect the beauty of Your creation, the seasons of our marriage reflect the intricate tapestry of our shared lives.

As we contemplate the current season of our marriage, we acknowledge the challenges and blessings it holds. In times of growth, help us remain grounded and open to the changes that spring brings. In the warmth of companionship, guard our hearts against complacency, and grant us the wisdom to continue nurturing our connection. In seasons of change and introspection, may we find solace in Your presence and guidance. And in times of challenge, may we draw closer to each other and to You for strength and comfort.

We seek Your wisdom in recognizing the lessons and opportunities each season offers. Just as You have provided for the earth in every season, we trust that You will provide for our marriage. Grant us the grace to embrace each season wholeheartedly, knowing that Your love and guidance are unwavering.

Lord, help us approach the different seasons of our marriage with patience, understanding, and unwavering faith. Just as You orchestrate the changing seasons of the earth, we trust You to guide us through the changing seasons of our relationship. Teach us to find joy in the unique beauty of each season and to see the fingerprints of Your love in every challenge and triumph.

May our marriage reflect the goodness and faithfulness that You display in the changing tapestry of creation. We pray that our love will grow deeper and our bond will strengthen as we weather the storms and bask in the sunshine of life together. May Your light shine upon us in every season, illuminating the path of love and grace that we walk hand in hand.

In Your name, we pray.

Amen.

Closing Thoughts:

As you journey through the seasons of your marriage, remember that each phase is a precious chapter in the story you're writing together. Just as the earth transitions from one season to another, so do you transition through various stages of love, growth, and challenge. By embracing the lessons and blessings of each season, you fortify the foundation of your marriage and create a legacy of love that will withstand the test of time. Just as the psalmist invites you to "taste and see that the Lord is good," taste and see that the journey of marriage, in all its seasons, is a journey worth savoring.

STRENGTHENING YOUR PRAYER LIFE TOGETHER

Scripture: Philippians 4:6

Do not be anxious about anything, but in everything by prayer and supplication with thanksgiving let your requests be made known to God.

Devotion:

Life often rushes by in a whirlwind of responsibilities, commitments, and demands. In the midst of this busyness, it's easy to overlook one of the most profound tools for deepening your connection as a couple and enriching your spiritual journey: prayer. This week, let's explore the transformative power of praying together and how it can infuse your marriage with a renewed sense of unity and purpose.

Reflection:

Pause for a moment and reflect on your journey of faith together. Have you and your spouse been intentional about nurturing a shared prayer life, or have you been navigating your spiritual paths individually? Openly discuss your experiences and thoughts about prayer, addressing any potential barriers that may have hindered your joint prayer practice.

Consider the beauty of praying together as an act of vulnerability and intimacy. Sharing your heart's desires, concerns, and gratitude with each other and with God creates a sacred bond that goes beyond words. Have a heartfelt conversation about your desires for a deeper connection through prayer and explore practical ways to make this a reality.

Imagine the impact of lifting each other in prayer during moments of joy and challenge. When one of you is facing a difficult decision or experiencing a triumph, the support of your partner's prayers can provide comfort and encouragement. Likewise, when you come together to intercede for your marriage and family, you're inviting God's presence to guide you through every step of your journey.

FOR HIM

FOR HER

Marriage Activity:

Dive into the world of prayer as a couple by exploring various forms and practices. Set aside time to read and meditate on a meaningful passage of Scripture. Consider praying through a psalm, allowing its words to express the emotions of your hearts. Experiment with writing down your prayers in a shared journal, providing a tangible record of your spiritual journey together.

Spontaneous prayer is another way to connect intimately with each other and with God. In unscripted moments, share your thoughts, worries, and joys in prayer. Additionally, try engaging in gratitude exercises, where you express thanks for the blessings in your lives. Through these practices, you'll uncover new dimensions of prayer that resonate with your unique journey.

PRAYER:

Heavenly Father,

We humbly come before You as a couple seeking to strengthen our bond through the power of prayer. Thank You for the gift of communication with You, a privilege that deepens our connection and enriches our faith journey. As we embark on this new season of praying together, we invite Your presence to guide us.

Grant us the courage to open our hearts to one another, to share our dreams, concerns, and longings in the safety of your loving embrace. Help us to create an environment where vulnerability is welcomed, and our souls are laid bare before You. May our shared prayers be a source of comfort, healing, and unity, drawing us closer to each other and to You.

Lord, teach us the art of listening in prayer. May we not only voice our thoughts but also attune our hearts to hear Your gentle whispers. As we explore different forms of prayer, may we discover the richness and diversity of ways to connect with You. Through our joint exploration, may our relationship grow stronger, and our intimacy deepen.

May the act of praying together become a cornerstone of our marriage, a practice that nourishes our souls and grounds our love in the unchanging truth of Your presence. May our prayers not only uplift us but also be a source of blessing for those around us.

In Jesus' name, we pray.

Amen.

Closing Thoughts:

As you embrace the journey of praying together, remember that prayer is both a conversation and an invitation. It's an opportunity to speak your heart and listen to the heartbeat of God. Just as you walk hand in hand through the seasons of life, you can also walk hand in hand in prayer, drawing strength, wisdom, and grace from the One who listens attentively. Let the bond of shared prayer become a testament to your commitment to each other and to the Creator, who weaves your stories together.

CULTIVATING A SERVANT'S HEART

Scripture: Galatians 5:13

For you were called to freedom, brothers. Only do not use your freedom as an opportunity for the flesh, but through love serve one another.

Devotion:

Marriage is a sacred union, a partnership bound by love and commitment. But at the core of this partnership lies a powerful truth often overlooked: the call to serve one another selflessly. In a world that often emphasizes individualism, embracing the role of a servant might seem counterintuitive. However, it is through this act of humble service that we can uncover the true depth and beauty of love in marriage.

Reflection:

Take a moment to reflect on the idea of serving one another in your marriage. What does it mean to be a servant to your spouse? It's more than just performing household chores or meeting each other's needs; it's about embodying a spirit of selflessness that seeks to uplift, encourage, and support your partner in every facet of life.

As you ponder this, consider the simple yet profound ways you can infuse your marriage with acts of service. It could be as straightforward as making your partner's favorite meal after a long day or taking the time to listen attentively when they need to talk. These small acts, fuelled by love, have the power to nurture the bond between you and create an environment of mutual care.

Spiritual Practice:

This week, as we delve into the theme of cultivating a servant's heart, let's embark on a journey of spiritual practice that embodies the essence of selfless service. While fasting is often associated with abstaining from food, it can also extend to other areas of our lives. In this practice, we'll explore fasting in a unique way—one that not only draws us closer to God but also nurtures the servant's heart within our marriage.

Consider what activities or habits you both engage in that consume a significant portion of your time and attention. It could be social media, television, excessive work, or a hobby that you both enjoy. These are areas where we often invest ourselves, sometimes without realizing how much of our lives they consume.

As a couple, take time to identify one activity or habit that you both can fast from for this week. The goal isn't just to abstain from these activities, but to intentionally replace that time with practices that align with a servant's heart. Instead of scrolling through social media, binge-watching TV shows, or dedicating extra hours to a hobby, choose to devote that time to seeking God's presence and growing together as a couple.

As you fast from the chosen activity, invest that reclaimed time into activities that foster spiritual growth. Spend time in prayer, both individually and together. Seek God's guidance for ways you can serve one another and those around you. Engage in Bible study, delving into passages that highlight the beauty of humility and servitude. Meditate on God's Word, allowing its truths to reshape your hearts and minds.

The remarkable aspect of this practice is that you're not only growing spiritually as individuals but also deepening your connection as a couple. Share your insights, reflections, and newfound understanding with each other. Discuss how the practice is challenging you to adopt a servant's heart in your daily interactions.

By engaging in this unique form of fasting, you're embodying the essence of a servant's heart. Just as you've chosen to give up something that may have held significance in your lives, you're symbolizing the willingness to lay aside personal desires for the greater good of your marriage. This act of selflessness not only strengthens your bond but also reflects the love of Christ, who laid down His life in service to humanity.

PRAYER:

Heavenly Father,

In the journey of our marriage, we come before You with hearts open to the transformative power of a servant's heart. Help us to embrace the humility that comes from serving one another, just as Your Son, Jesus Christ, humbly served those around Him.

As we seek to love each other more deeply, grant us the wisdom to recognize the needs of our partner. May we be attuned to their joys, struggles, and desires, offering our hands and hearts in service. Strengthen our commitment to support each other selflessly, demonstrating Your love through our actions.

In moments of weariness or selfishness, remind us of Your perfect example of love—the sacrificial love that serves without reservation. Teach us to lay down our own needs and desires for the sake of our partner's well-being. May our marriage be a testament to the beautiful dance of give and take, of lifting each other up.

Lord, help us overcome pride and any obstacles that hinder our willingness to serve. Grant us the grace to cultivate a servant's heart, one that reflects Your love and grace. As we serve one another, may our marriage flourish, and may our actions be a reflection of Your unwavering love.

In Jesus' name, we pray.

Amen.

Closing Thoughts:

Cultivating a servant's heart within your marriage is a transformative journey that leads to greater intimacy and connection. As you actively seek out opportunities to serve and support each other, you're not only fostering a strong partnership but also leaving a legacy of love for generations to come. By embracing the call to serve, you're weaving threads of selflessness, humility, and compassion into the very fabric of your relationship. Just as Christ's love was marked by service, may your marriage shine as a beacon of love, reflecting the beauty of a servant's heart.

FINDING BALANCE IN TECHNOLOGY USE

Scripture: Psalm 46:10

Be still, and know that I am God. I will be exalted among the nations, I will be exalted in the earth!

Devotion:

In today's digital age, technology has become an integral part of our lives, connecting us in ways unimaginable before. It has enhanced communication, productivity, and entertainment, yet it also brings with it challenges that can impact our relationships, especially within the context of marriage. This week, let's explore the theme of finding balance in technology use and its profound influence on our marital bond.

In our quest for balance, it's essential to acknowledge the role that technology plays in our lives. Whether it's staying connected through messaging apps, social media, or the allure of endless streaming content, these digital experiences can enrich our lives but also threaten to disconnect us from our immediate surroundings, including our spouses.

Technology can be a tool for connection, but it can also inadvertently foster disconnection if not managed mindfully. As a couple, take time to recognize the ways in which technology has positively impacted your relationship and where it might have posed challenges. By acknowledging both the benefits and potential drawbacks, you lay the foundation for intentional and healthy technology use.

Reflection:

Take time as a couple to reflect on your technology habits. Are there times when your focus on screens has come at the expense of quality time together? How do you respond to notifications or messages during shared moments? Reflecting on these questions can be an eye-opening experience. Remember, the goal isn't to demonize technology but to ensure it enhances rather than detracts from your marriage.

Think of technology as a guest at the table of your relationship. Just as guests enhance our gatherings without becoming the sole focus, technology should complement your interactions without overshadowing the moments you share. Consider establishing guidelines or boundaries that promote balance. For instance, designate certain times as "tech-free zones" to ensure uninterrupted connection, or agree to put away devices during meals and meaningful conversations.

Amid the constant digital noise, prioritizing quality time with your spouse has become more crucial than ever. Consider establishing tech-free zones or times in your daily routine, where your undivided attention is devoted to each other. Engage in meaningful conversations, participate in activities you both enjoy, and create cherished memories without the constant interruption of screens.

Imagine a weekend morning when you share a leisurely breakfast without the distraction of phones or tablets. Instead of scrolling through social media, you engage in genuine conversations about your hopes, dreams, and even your plans for the day. By intentionally creating these moments, you not only deepen your bond but also cultivate an environment where both of you feel valued and heard.

FOR HER

Marriage Activity:

This week, engage in activities that encourage meaningful connection. Whether it's cooking together, going for a walk, or participating in a hobby you both love, focus on the present moment. Share stories, dreams, and thoughts that might have gone unnoticed in the hum of everyday life. Use this time to deepen your understanding of one another and strengthen your bond.

Consider embarking on a joint project that requires teamwork and communication. This could be as simple as a home improvement task or as creative as starting a shared journal. The act of collaborating on something tangible underscores the beauty of being present and engaged with each other.

PRAYER:

Heavenly Father,

We come before you, seeking wisdom and guidance in navigating the digital age within our marriage. Help us to recognize the ways technology has enriched our lives while also acknowledging where it may have unintentionally created distance between us. Grant us discernment to know when to disconnect from screens and connect with each other more deeply.

Empower us to set healthy boundaries that prioritize quality time and meaningful conversations. May our use of technology always enhance our relationship rather than hinder it. In the midst of a constantly buzzing world, help us find quiet moments of togetherness and rediscover the joy of being fully present for one another.

In Jesus' name, we pray.

Amen.

Closing Thoughts:

In a world abuzz with notifications and updates, remember that the most precious gift you can give each other is your presence. The quiet moments, the uninterrupted conversations, and the shared experiences are what truly nourish your marriage. Striking a balance in technology use isn't about rejection; it's about embracing each other fully in the here and now.

As you find equilibrium in the digital landscape, you're cultivating a marriage that's resilient, vibrant, and rooted in the moments you choose to share. May your commitment to balance and your dedication to preserving the sacred spaces of your togetherness serve as a testimony to the enduring strength of your love.

BUILDING TRUST
THROUGH TRANSPARENCY

Scripture: Proverbs 28:13

Whoever conceals his transgressions will not prosper, but he who confesses and forsakes them will obtain mercy.

Devotion:

In the intricate dance of marriage, trust is the delicate thread that weaves hearts together. It's the cornerstone upon which lasting love and intimacy are built. Just as a foundation needs solid stones, trust requires the bricks of openness and transparency. This week, let's explore the profound theme of building trust through genuine honesty within your marriage.

Trust is more than a mere belief in the fidelity of your partner; it's a deep-seated assurance that you can count on each other's words, actions, and intentions. It's nurtured through consistent honesty and open communication. Just as a tree needs roots to stand tall, trust requires the roots of transparency to flourish.

Imagine trust as a garden. At its center is a well-tended flowerbed of transparency. Here, the seeds of truth are sown, watered by genuine conversations, and nurtured by vulnerability. Transparency requires a willingness to reveal your true thoughts, feelings, and experiences, even when they might be difficult to share. It's through this openness that the blooms of trust take root and flourish.

Reflection:

Take a reflective journey as a couple. Engage in a heartfelt conversation about the areas where more transparency is needed. Perhaps it's sharing your dreams and fears, discussing past mistakes, or revealing concerns that have been kept hidden. As you both open up, remember that this isn't about blame or judgment; it's about fostering an environment where truth can thrive.

Think about moments when you might have concealed your emotions or thoughts. Reflect on why these moments occurred and how they impacted your connection. This reflection isn't meant to bring guilt but to illuminate areas where more transparency can bring healing and growth.

Transparency is a choice, one that requires courage and vulnerability. It's about making the conscious decision to be honest even when it's uncomfortable. This commitment can reshape the landscape of your relationship, fostering an atmosphere of trust and intimacy. As you commit to transparency, you're making room for authenticity, vulnerability, and the unwavering assurance that you're each other's safe haven.

Consider the moments when you've witnessed true transparency in action. Perhaps it was the sharing of a difficult truth that ultimately deepened your bond. Remember how that moment solidified your trust and made you feel more connected. Carry that memory as a reminder of the power of openness in your marriage.

Spiritual Practice:

As you embark on this journey of transparency, consider the role of faith in your commitment. Just as you entrust your hearts to each other, place your trust in God's guidance as well. Seek His wisdom in understanding the beauty and challenges of vulnerability. Pray for the strength to lay bare your thoughts and emotions, knowing that true healing and growth often stem from these moments of honesty.

PRAYER:

Heavenly Father,

We come before you, seeking your guidance and strength in building trust through honesty within our marriage. Help us to recognize the areas where more transparency is needed, and grant us the courage to share our thoughts, feelings, and experiences openly.

May our commitment to transparency deepen our connection and foster an atmosphere of trust and intimacy. As we open ourselves to each other, may we also open ourselves to your wisdom and guidance. Thank you for the gift of vulnerability, which allows us to grow individually and as a couple.

In Jesus' name, we pray.

Amen.

Closing Thoughts:

As you journey through this week, remember that transparency isn't just about sharing facts; it's about unveiling the essence of who you are. Each conversation, each truth shared, is a thread that weaves a tapestry of trust. Every moment of openness strengthens your connection, adding color and depth to your marriage's fabric.

Transparency isn't always easy, but it's a gift you give each other. It's an invitation to understand and be understood, to support and be supported. By committing to honesty, you're sowing the seeds of a lasting connection built on trust, a connection that will weather storms and bask in the sunshine of shared truth.

143

EMBRACING DIVERSITY IN YOUR MARRIAGE

Scripture: Galatians 3:28

There is neither Jew nor Greek, there is neither slave nor free, there is no male and female, for you are all one in Christ Jesus.

Devotion:

Marriage is a beautiful union of two souls, each with its own story, culture, and experiences. Just as the colors of a rainbow come together to create a breath-taking spectrum, so too do your unique backgrounds blend to form the vibrant tapestry of your relationship. This week, let's explore the richness of embracing diversity and cultural differences within your marriage.

Reflection:

God's creation is marked by diversity, from the myriad of landscapes to the countless faces that populate the world. Your marriage is a microcosm of this divine tapestry, reflecting the various hues of your individual experiences. Like a mosaic, your diverse backgrounds create a picture that is far more intricate and beautiful than either of you could be alone.

Take a moment to reflect on the cultural elements that each of you brings to the relationship. From traditions to languages, from cuisine to celebrations, these are the threads that make up the fabric of your marriage. Embracing diversity doesn't mean losing your individual identities; it means celebrating them as part of a shared journey.

Each culture carries its own stories, values, and wisdom. Embracing diversity within your marriage offers an incredible opportunity for learning and growth. Take time to delve into each other's cultural backgrounds, sharing stories of family traditions, childhood memories, and cultural celebrations. As you learn, you deepen your understanding of your partner's roots and the experiences that have shaped them.

Consider the parallels between embracing diversity in your marriage and your journey of faith. Just as God's family encompasses believers from every nation and culture, your marriage is an opportunity to experience unity in the midst of beautiful diversity. This shared journey can foster growth, empathy, and a deep appreciation for the unique perspectives you both bring to the table.

Marriage Activity:

Imagine your marriage as a canvas, waiting to be painted with the vibrant colors of your combined backgrounds. Share your cultural celebrations with each other and invite unity by participating in them together. Celebrate holidays, festivals, and traditions from each other's cultures, creating memories that are uniquely your own.

Take a moment to reflect on the ways your diverse backgrounds have already enriched your relationship. Consider how your different perspectives have brought new insights and ideas, fostering a deeper connection between you. Each story shared, each meal enjoyed, and each tradition celebrated is a brushstroke on the canvas of your marriage, creating a masterpiece of unity in diversity.

PRAYER:

Heavenly Father,

We come before you with hearts filled with gratitude for the beautiful diversity you have woven into our marriage. Just as you have crafted the world with a kaleidoscope of cultures and experiences, you have brought us together, two individuals with unique backgrounds and stories. We thank you for the richness that these differences bring to our relationship.

Lord, help us to navigate the complexities of diversity with wisdom and grace. May we always approach each other's cultures and traditions with open hearts and a genuine desire to learn and understand. Let us not merely tolerate our differences but truly celebrate them, recognizing that they are a reflection of your boundless creativity.

In the moments where misunderstandings arise due to cultural nuances, grant us patience and humility to seek understanding. Remind us that through dialogue and curiosity, we can bridge gaps and grow closer as we uncover the treasures of each other's worlds.

We pray for unity in our diversity, Lord. Let our marriage be a testament to the power of love and respect that transcends cultural boundaries. May our relationship be a safe space where we can be our authentic selves without fear of judgment. Allow us to appreciate the strengths that each of us brings from our backgrounds, and grant us the wisdom to navigate any challenges that may arise.

As we continue this journey together, Lord, infuse our marriage with the beauty of our combined cultures. May our home be a place where traditions are celebrated, stories are shared, and memories are created. Just as you have designed the body of Christ to be a diverse and unified entity, help us embrace the diversity in our marriage and celebrate it as a reflection of your love.

Guide us, Heavenly Father, to weave the threads of our backgrounds into a tapestry of unity, strength, and beauty. May our love story resonate with the harmonious blend of our cultures, creating a melody that glorifies you and brings joy to our hearts.

In Jesus' name, we pray.

Amen.

Closing Thoughts:

As you walk this path of embracing diversity, remember that your marriage is a harmonious melody composed of different notes and rhythms. Each cultural aspect contributes to the depth and beauty of the song you're creating together. Just as a symphony becomes more powerful when each instrument plays its part, your marriage flourishes when you both bring your unique backgrounds to the forefront.

In a world where differences can sometimes divide, your marriage stands as a testament to the beauty of unity through diversity. The cultures you represent merge to form a stronger, more resilient bond. As you continue to celebrate your individual backgrounds within the safe haven of your relationship, you create a melody that resonates with love, respect, and a deeper understanding of God's diverse and wondrous creation.

THE ART OF APOLOGIZING

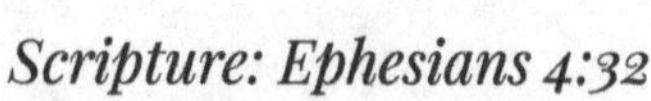

Scripture: Ephesians 4:32

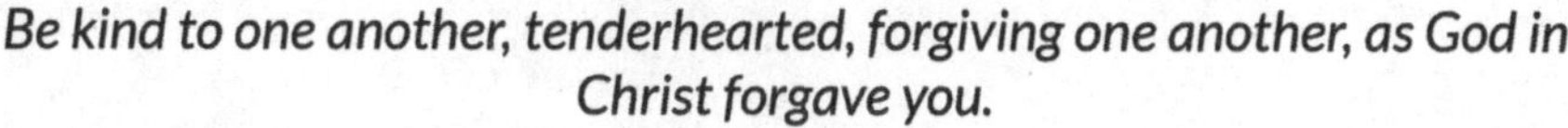

Be kind to one another, tenderhearted, forgiving one another, as God in Christ forgave you.

Devotion:

Apologizing is an art that requires humility, vulnerability, and a genuine desire for healing. In the journey of marriage, disagreements and misunderstandings are inevitable, and with them comes the opportunity to practice the art of apologizing. Just as God's grace and forgiveness are extended to us, we are called to mirror that grace within our relationships.

Apologizing is not a sign of weakness but a reflection of the strength of your commitment to your spouse and your marriage. It takes courage to admit when we're wrong, to recognize the hurt we may have caused, and to take responsibility for our actions. This act of vulnerability opens the door to healing and restoration.

Reflect on the times when you've had difficulty apologizing. What held you back? Pride, fear of vulnerability, or a misunderstanding of the true purpose of an apology? Remember that apologizing isn't just about admitting fault; it's about valuing the relationship more than your ego.

Reflection:

Forgiveness is not just a gift we give to our spouse; it's also a responsibility we hold to ourselves and to God. Holding onto grudges and unresolved conflicts can poison the atmosphere of your marriage and hinder your spiritual growth. As you reflect on forgiveness, consider the weight it lifts off your shoulders when you choose to let go of resentment and anger.

Think about the times you've been forgiven by God. His mercy is boundless, and His forgiveness is a gift that restores us to Him. In the same way, when we forgive our spouse, we create an environment where healing can take place, and love can flourish once again.

Spiritual Practice:

One beautiful way to deepen your understanding of forgiveness and practice the art of apologizing is through communion. Just as Christ forgave us through His sacrifice, we can use this sacred act to remember His grace and apply it to our relationships.

Take time to share communion together. As you break bread and drink from the cup, reflect on Christ's ultimate act of forgiveness. Let this act of remembrance guide your hearts toward a deeper understanding of the forgiveness you're called to extend and receive in your marriage.

As you partake in communion, confess any lingering resentment, hurt, or unforgiveness you may be holding onto. Use this moment to apologize to each other for any wrongs you've committed and to ask for forgiveness. Embrace the powerful symbolism of Christ's sacrifice and the redemption it offers to your marriage.

PRAYER:

Heavenly Father,

We come before You with hearts humbled by Your boundless grace and forgiveness. Thank You for showing us the way to true reconciliation through the sacrifice of Your Son, Jesus Christ. As we reflect on the art of apologizing and the power of forgiveness in our marriage, we seek Your guidance and strength.

Lord, help us recognize the importance of apologizing sincerely and seeking forgiveness wholeheartedly. Grant us the courage to admit our wrongs, to lay down our pride, and to extend apologies with genuine hearts. May our apologies become bridges to healing, and may our humility bring restoration to any wounds in our relationship.

As we partake in communion, we remember the ultimate act of forgiveness through the body and blood of Christ. May this sacred moment deepen our understanding of Your grace and inspire us to mirror that grace within our marriage. As we confess our shortcomings and ask for forgiveness from one another, let Your presence fill our hearts with humility and love.

Father, teach us to forgive as You forgive, with open hearts and without holding onto grudges. Help us to release any resentment or anger, allowing Your love to flow freely in our marriage. Strengthen us to uphold the value of forgiveness, even when it's challenging.

Lord, we thank You for the gift of forgiveness, for the chance to start anew, and for the hope of restoring relationships. May our marriage be a living testament to Your grace, reflecting the beauty of Your forgiveness to the world around us.

In the name of Jesus, who taught us the power of forgiveness, we pray.

Amen.

Closing Thoughts:

In marriage, the art of apologizing becomes a testament to your commitment to each other and to the God who unconditionally forgives us. Just as Christ's sacrifice brings reconciliation and restoration, your willingness to apologize and forgive fosters an environment of healing and growth.

Apologizing doesn't diminish your value; it enhances your character and strengthens the bond you share. As you continue to practice the art of apologizing, remember that forgiveness is a key component of the love that sustains your marriage. With each apology offered and forgiveness granted, you breathe new life into your relationship, demonstrating the grace and love that reflects God's heart.

Let the art of apologizing be a cornerstone of your marriage, a testament to your commitment, and a mirror of the forgiveness that Christ offers to each of us. May your willingness to seek and extend forgiveness be a reflection of God's transforming love, shining brightly in your marriage journey.

SAVORING THE
SIMPLE MOMENTS

Scripture: Ecclesiastes 5:18

Behold, what I have seen to be good and fitting is to eat and drink and find enjoyment in all the toil with which one toils under the sun the few days of his life that God has given him, for this is his lot.

Devotion:

In the hustle and bustle of our lives, it's easy to overlook the simple moments that truly make life beautiful. We often find ourselves chasing after grand experiences, while the ordinary moments, infused with love and meaning, slip through our fingers. As we journey through marriage, let's take a moment to reflect on the art of savoring the simple moments that grace our everyday lives.

Life is a tapestry woven with both extraordinary events and mundane routines. Yet, it's often the simplest moments that hold the most profound meaning. In the embrace of a morning hug, the laughter shared over a cup of coffee, or the comfort of holding hands during an evening walk, we find glimpses of true joy. These are the moments that form the backbone of our daily lives, and in their simplicity, they hold immeasurable significance.

When we slow down and intentionally appreciate these moments, we discover that they carry the power to nurture our marriage. The sparkle in our partner's eyes, the warmth of their smile, the sound of their laughter—these are the treasures that create a bond that withstands the test of time. By intentionally savoring these everyday instances, we open ourselves to a deeper connection and a heightened sense of gratitude.

Reflection:

Consider the last time you shared a quiet moment with your spouse—a shared glance that communicated more than words ever could, or a spontaneous dance in the living room. These moments are like the hidden gems in the rough; they're easy to overlook, yet they hold immense beauty. Take a moment to reflect on these instances and recognize how they've added richness to your marriage.

Discuss with your spouse how you can intentionally cultivate a spirit of gratitude for these simple moments. Share your thoughts on the moments that have brought you the most joy recently. By acknowledging and appreciating these instances together, you deepen your connection and create a shared treasure trove of memories.

FOR HER

Marriage Activity:

This week, embark on a journey to intentionally create a simple yet beautiful moment together. It could be as uncomplicated as preparing a meal together, having a spontaneous picnic, or stargazing on a clear night. The key is to fully engage in the experience, relishing each moment and allowing it to imprint on your hearts.

As part of this activity, consider extending joy to others. Choose a simple act of kindness or service that you can do together. Whether it's volunteering at a local charity, surprising a neighbor with a thoughtful gesture, or spending time with an elderly relative, your joint effort can amplify the joy and meaning of the moment. As you give to others, you'll find that your own joy is multiplied.

PRAYER:

Heavenly Father,

We come before You with hearts full of gratitude for the simple moments that bring joy to our marriage. In a world that often rushes by, we thank You for the beauty found in the ordinary—a gentle touch, a shared smile, a heartfelt conversation. These moments remind us of the depth of our love and the blessings You've bestowed upon us.

As we intentionally savor these simple moments, may our hearts be filled with gratitude. Help us to recognize the beauty in each day and to find joy in the little things. May these moments knit us closer together and create lasting memories that we can treasure.

Guide us as we embark on the activity of creating a simple moment together and sharing that joy with others. May it be a reflection of the love and appreciation we hold for each other and the community around us. And as we share these experiences, may they become the building blocks of a marriage that is rich in love and laughter.

In Your precious name, we pray.

Amen.

Closing Thoughts:

As we journey through life, let us not underestimate the value of the simple moments. These instances, often overlooked, hold the power to infuse our days with joy and meaning. By intentionally embracing and cherishing them, we create a reservoir of shared memories that fortify our marriage and remind us of the beauty in the everyday.

ENCOURAGING YOUR SPOUSE'S DREAMS

Scripture: Philippians 2:3

Do nothing from selfish ambition or conceit, but in humility count others more significant than yourselves.

Devotion:

In the tapestry of marriage, each partner brings their unique aspirations, dreams, and passions. a marriage becomes truly vibrant when both individuals not only pursue their own dreams but also actively encourage and support each other's aspirations. This week, let's delve into the art of being a supportive partner who stands as a cheerleader and an unwavering pillar for your spouse's dreams.

Our dreams are like individual notes that, when combined, create a harmonious symphony. When we commit to encouraging and nurturing each other's dreams, we contribute to this beautiful melody that resonates throughout our marriage. As we embark on this journey, let's reflect on how we can foster an environment where our partner's dreams can flourish.

Often, in the busyness of life, it's easy to overlook the dreams and passions that make our spouse unique. However, the foundation of a strong partnership lies in recognizing the significance of each other's aspirations. Whether it's a career goal, a creative pursuit, or a personal achievement, these dreams shape our identity and contribute to our happiness.

Reflection:

Take a moment to discuss your dreams and goals with your spouse. Create an open and non-judgmental space where you can openly share your aspirations. Listen attentively to each other's dreams and discuss how you can actively support and encourage one another in their pursuit.

Reflect on how you can become a spiritual encourager for your spouse's dreams. Being a spiritual encourager means not only offering words of support but also aligning your actions with your partner's aspirations. It involves acknowledging their passions, discussing potential challenges, and brainstorming strategies together.

Spiritual Practice:

Learn to be a spiritual encourager to your spouse. In order to do so, consider these practices:

• Active Listening: Pay attention when your spouse talks about their dreams. Engage in conversations that delve deeper into their desires and plans. Ask questions that show your genuine interest and understanding.

• Affirming Words: Speak words of affirmation and belief in your spouse's dreams. Offer genuine compliments and praise for their talents and efforts. Remind them of their capabilities and strengths.

• Prayerful Support: Lift your spouse's dreams in prayer. Ask God to guide and bless their endeavors. Pray for their courage, resilience, and success. Praying together can create a powerful spiritual connection.

• Taking Action: Look for practical ways to support your spouse's dreams. Whether it's setting aside time for them to work on their goals, offering a helping hand, or connecting them with resources, your actions can speak volumes.

• Celebrating Milestones: Rejoice in your spouse's achievements, both big and small. Celebrate milestones together and acknowledge the progress they've made. Your encouragement can boost their motivation.

PRAYER:

Heavenly Father,

We come before You with hearts full of gratitude for the dreams and aspirations You've placed in our hearts. We thank You for the gift of marriage—a partnership where we can grow, learn, and support each other's dreams.

As we journey together, help us to become spiritual encouragers for one another. May our words and actions reflect our belief in each other's potential. Guide us in creating an environment where our dreams can thrive, and our aspirations can take flight.

Grant us the wisdom to actively listen, the strength to offer unwavering support, and the humility to celebrate each other's successes. We pray for Your guidance as we navigate challenges and pursue our dreams side by side.

In Your name, we pray.

Amen.

Closing Thoughts:

As we commit to becoming spiritual encouragers for each other's dreams, we contribute to a marriage that thrives on mutual support and shared aspirations. By actively nurturing each other's passions and goals, we create a partnership that not only strengthens our bond but also encourages personal growth. As you embrace each other's dreams, remember that your partnership becomes a canvas where both of your unique aspirations come together to create a masterpiece of love, support, and shared accomplishments.

FACING THE FUTURE WITH HOPE

Scripture: Jeremiah 29:11

For I know the plans I have for you, declares the Lord, plans for welfare and not for evil, to give you a future and a hope.

Devotion:

In the journey of marriage, the future holds a tapestry of moments yet to be woven, dreams yet to be realized, and challenges yet to be overcome. It's a journey of unknowns, but one thing remains certain: as we face the future together, we do so with hope. This week, let's explore the beauty of hope and the assurance that God's plans for us are filled with goodness.

The future is a vast expanse of uncertainty, yet it's also a canvas onto which we can paint our dreams and aspirations. The foundation of our hope is anchored in our trust in God's plan for us. As we look forward, let's reflect on how we can cultivate a hopeful mindset and embrace the journey ahead.

In the midst of life's twists and turns, it's easy to be consumed by worry and anxiety about what lies ahead. However, God's promise in Jeremiah 29:11 reminds us that His plans for us are ones of welfare, not of harm. As we navigate the future, let's remember that our hope rests not in our own abilities, but in the knowledge that we are held in the palm of God's hand.

Reflection:

Take a moment to sit down with your spouse and discuss your hopes and dreams for the future. What aspirations do you both hold dear? What goals do you want to achieve together? Consider these hopes as "anchors" for your journey. An anchor is something that provides stability and direction. Just as a ship uses an anchor to stay grounded in the midst of storms, these anchors will guide your decisions and actions as you move toward your desired future.

As you explore these dreams and anchors, think about how they align with God's plan for your life. Invite His guidance into your discussions, seeking His wisdom in your plans.

For Him

For Her

Marriage Activity:

This week, embark on a journey of setting powerful anchors for your marriage. Choose a few of your shared dreams and aspirations that you both feel passionate about. These dreams will become your "anchors" – the guiding principles that shape your decisions, actions, and the course of your life together.

For each anchor, brainstorm practical steps you can take to move closer to that dream. Consider how your career choices, life decisions, and daily actions can be aligned with these anchors. Creating a roadmap toward your anchors will provide you with a sense of purpose and direction, helping you navigate the future with intention and hope.

PRAYER:

Heavenly Father,

As we stand on the threshold of the future, we come before You with hearts filled with hope and trust. We thank You for the promise of Jeremiah 29:11, a promise that assures us of Your plans for our welfare and a future filled with hope. In a world of uncertainties, we find solace in Your unwavering love and guidance.

Lord, as we explore our dreams and set powerful anchors for our journey as a couple, we invite Your presence into our discussions and decisions. May our anchors be rooted in Your will for our lives, aligning our aspirations with Your perfect plan. Help us to prioritize the dreams that reflect Your purpose for us, and guide us in mapping out practical steps to achieve them.

We recognize that the path ahead may hold challenges and unexpected turns, but we find strength in knowing that You are our anchor in the storm. Grant us the courage to face the future with unwavering hope, trusting that Your hand guides our every step. As we work together to bring our dreams to fruition, may we always be mindful of Your presence, seeking Your wisdom and direction.

Lord, as we embark on this journey of setting anchors, we commit our plans into Your hands. May our marriage be a testament to Your faithfulness and goodness, reflecting the hope that comes from walking in alignment with Your purposes. As we navigate the seas of life, may our hearts be steadfast in the assurance that You are the Captain of our ship, guiding us toward a future filled with purpose, joy, and the realization of our shared dreams.

In Jesus' name, we pray.

Amen.

Closing Thoughts:

As you set these powerful anchors, remember that God's promise in Jeremiah 29:11 remains the ultimate source of your hope. By aligning your dreams with His plan, you can move forward confidently, knowing that your steps are guided by a divine purpose. Just as an anchor steadies a ship amidst the currents, your anchors will keep you focused on your journey, even in the face of challenges. May your marriage be a testament to the hope that rests in knowing that God's plans for you are filled with goodness, purpose, and the promise of a future that is held secure in His loving hands.

REFLECTING ON YOUR MARRIAGE JOURNEY

Scripture: Psalm 105:5

Remember the wondrous works that he has done, his miracles, and the judgments he uttered.

Devotion:

As you stand at the threshold of completing a year-long journey through the various aspects of marriage, it's fitting to pause and reflect. This final week invites you to look back at the path you've traveled, the lessons learned, the joys experienced, and the challenges overcome. Just as the psalmist encourages us to remember God's wondrous works, take this time to remember the journey you and your spouse embarked upon, the milestones you reached, and the growth you achieved.

Reflecting on your marriage journey is a powerful way to honor the faithfulness of God in your lives. Throughout this year, you've delved into numerous topics, scriptures, and practices that have enriched your relationship. As you contemplate the highs and lows, the laughter and tears, remember that God has been with you every step of the way. He has been the silent partner in every discussion, the source of strength in every trial, and the reason for every smile shared.

Your journey together is a testament to God's provision, His guidance, and His unwavering love. Just as Psalm 105:5 encourages us to remember His miracles and wondrous works, remember the times when His presence was palpable, the moments when His wisdom guided your decisions, and the instances when His grace carried you through challenges.

Reflection:

As you reflect on your marriage journey, take a moment to appreciate the tapestry that has been woven. Recall the times when you leaned on each other, the instances when you grew closer in adversity, and the occasions when you celebrated in unity. Recognize the threads of patience, forgiveness, communication, and love that have been intricately woven to create the beautiful fabric of your partnership.

Acknowledge the growth you've experienced individually and as a couple. Reflect on the lessons you've learned about communication, trust, intimacy, and selflessness. Just as a tapestry tells a story through its intricate patterns, your marriage journey tells a story of commitment, transformation, and God's grace at work.

Spiritual Practice:

As you conclude this year of growth and exploration in your marriage, dedicate time to reflect on the hand of God in your journey. Find a quiet space where you and your spouse can sit down together. Take out a journal and write down the highs and lows you've experienced as a couple throughout the year. Be open and honest about the challenges you faced, the victories you celebrated, and the moments that brought you closer to each other and to God.

As you reflect, see how God's presence was woven into each chapter of your journey. Look for His fingerprints in the moments of joy and in the moments of struggle. Consider how His Word and the spiritual practices you engaged in impacted your relationship. Take time to express gratitude for His faithfulness and provision.

PRAYER:

Heavenly Father,

As we stand on the threshold of completing a year-long journey through the intricacies of marriage, we bow in humble gratitude before Your presence. You have been the constant companion, the unwavering guide, and the source of strength throughout this incredible journey. As we reflect on the path we've walked, we're reminded of Your faithfulness and love that have carried us through every season.

Lord, we thank You for the highs that made us soar with joy and the lows that deepened our trust in You and in each other. We praise You for the moments of laughter that filled our hearts with gladness and the tears that brought us closer as we leaned on Your promises. Every twist and turn, every trial and triumph, has been a thread woven into the beautiful tapestry of our marriage, and for that, we are immensely grateful.

As we take this time to remember, we're in awe of Your guidance that directed our steps, Your wisdom that shaped our decisions, and Your grace that sustained us through challenges. Help us recognize Your fingerprints on each moment, Your love in every interaction, and Your light that has illuminated our path.

In the quiet moments of reflection, Lord, reveal to us the lessons You intended for us to learn. Show us the ways in which Your Word has transformed our hearts and deepened our understanding of each other. Let Your Spirit remind us of the times when we leaned on You for strength and found comfort in Your presence.

As we move forward, may the tapestry of our journey be a vivid reminder of Your enduring faithfulness. With hearts filled with gratitude, we step into the future with renewed hope and trust. Just as Psalm 105:5 encourages us to remember Your wondrous works, we commit to remembering the journey You've led us on and to continue growing in Your love.

In Jesus' name, we pray,

Amen.

Closing Thoughts:

As you reflect on the journey you've undertaken this past year, may you be filled with gratitude for the growth and blessings you've experienced. Every devotional, every scripture, and every practice has contributed to shaping your marriage into a stronger, more resilient bond.

As you close this chapter of exploration and reflection, step into the coming year with a heart full of gratitude and a deep awareness of God's presence in your relationship. Just as Psalm 105:5 invites us to remember the wondrous works of God, remember the wondrous works He has done in your marriage. Celebrate the journey you've taken together, and may it continue to be a testament to His faithfulness for years to come.

CONCLUSION

As we come to the conclusion of this year-long journey of marriage devotionals, we want to express our heartfelt gratitude for joining us on this path of growth, reflection, and spiritual connection. Throughout these weeks, we have explored various facets of a thriving marriage, seeking wisdom from God's Word and applying it to our lives.

As couples, we've delved into the depths of love, forgiveness, communication, intimacy, and so much more. We've taken intentional steps to build a foundation that honors God and nurtures our relationship. Each week, we've uncovered new insights and tools to strengthen our bond, reminding ourselves that marriage is not just a union between two people, but a partnership woven together by the divine.

In the span of a year, we've discovered that a God-centered marriage is an ongoing journey of learning, growing, and leaning into His grace. We've celebrated moments of joy and navigated challenges with faith. We've strived to cultivate qualities like patience, kindness, and humility, recognizing that these attributes reflect the character of Christ.

As we conclude this series, let us remember that the journey doesn't end here. Marriage is a lifelong commitment, and our growth as individuals and as a couple is continuous. The devotionals we've shared are not just words on a page; they are invitations to apply timeless truths to our daily lives, enriching our marriage and glorifying God.

Let's carry the lessons we've learned and the practices we've embraced into the future. Let's approach each day with renewed dedication to love, serve, and honor each other. And above all, let's keep Christ at the center of our marriage, knowing that He is the anchor that holds us steady through every season.

As we move forward, let's be encouraged by the words of Philippians 1:6: "And I am sure of this, that he who began a good work in you will bring it to completion at the day of Jesus Christ." Let's continue to rely on God's grace and guidance, trusting that He will lead us to deeper intimacy, unshakeable unity, and a love that grows stronger with each passing year.

Thank you for walking this journey of marriage devotionals with us. May God bless your marriage abundantly, and may His love shine through every moment you share together.